Alf Townsend
The London Cabbie

Lincolnshire County Council	
AD 04409942	
Askews	
388.321	£7.99
	0815894/0021

The History Press

This book was first published
under the title *Cabbie* in 2003 by
Sutton Publishing Limited.

This paperback edition first published in 2007

Reprinted in 2008 by The History Press

British Library Cataloguing in Publication Data
A catalogue record for this book is available from the
British Library.

ISBN 978-0-7509-4496-0

Typeset in 12/14.5pt Photina.
Typesetting and origination by
Sutton Publishing Limited.
Printed and bound in England.

CONTENTS

FOREWORD

Alf Townsend has been associated with the cab trade press for as long as I can remember. He was a founder member of the LTDA (the Licensed Taxi Driver's Association), and first started writing articles for their publication, *Taxi Newspaper*, way back in the 1960s. Some years later, he was invited to join the newly launched *Taxi Globe*. He moved on to the *London Taxi Times*, then finally the *Cab Driver Newspaper*.

Alf always writes what he thinks is the truth and over the years his hard-hitting and down-to-earth comments have often upset many notables in the trade. But many of his regular readers enjoy his fortnightly humorous columns, forever cocking a snook at the establishment. He has always involved himself in the trade that he loves. For many years he played for the Mocatra (Motor Cab Trade) football team and later joined the newly formed Golf Society. He organised Cab Trade Golf Tournaments, gaining sponsorship from major companies and taking the qualifiers to Spain for a free golf holiday.

In the early 1990s, Alf was appointed as the senior LTDA Trade Rep. at Heathrow Airport. He helped to form the cab-drivers' cooperative, HALT (Heathrow Airport Licensed Taxis), and eventually became its Chairman. Alf then started the *HALT Magazine* and, almost unaided, produced and edited it for the next five years or more. The *HALT Magazine* became a popular, twenty-page, full-colour publication, which always showed a small profit.

In the late 1990s, Alf decided to give up all his political positions and concentrated instead on writing books. This book is his second effort and the first to be published.

Dave Allen
Editor, *Cab Driver Newspaper*

DEDICATION

This book is dedicated to the loving memory of our wonderful daughter Jenny, who tragically lost her painful, six-year battle against cancer on 27 December 1999. She was just one month past her forty-first birthday when she died. During those dark days, I wouldn't have been able to carry on without the deep love of my darling wife Nicolette and the support of the rest of our family: Jenny's caring husband Keith, their lovely son Sam, my son Nick, his wife Rose and their two children Ruben and Soela, and last but not least, the love and affection from my daughter Jo, husband Adam and their children, Charlie, Holly and the twins Albert and Jack. They all helped me to write this book.

'Your spirit is our strength, darling.'

ACKNOWLEDGEMENTS

My thanks to my friend and colleague Philip Warren, a well-known cab trade historian, for allowing me to quote extensively from his book *The History of the London Cab Trade, from 1600 to the Present Day*. Without his kind permission I wouldn't have been able to construct my chapter, 'From Horses to Horseless Carriages'. Also, a big thank-you to Philip for supplying me with many of the old photos from his extensive collection. Philip's book is well worth reading – especially if you are a history buff! My thanks also to Stuart Pessock, the editor of *Taxi Newspaper*, for letting me raid his photo collection and to my son Nick for taking the photos of Heathrow, the Knowledge Boys and the Cab Shelters. Thanks also to Malcolm Linskey, the 'boss-man' at the Knowledge Point School for the pics of the Knowledge Girls.

INTRODUCTION

It's been more than three decades since a book has been written about the famous London cabbie, so I thought it was time to write another. To be perfectly honest, my dear wife has been nagging me for a long time to get on with it! That first book, written by the late Maurice Levinson – my very first editor when I became a trade journalist at 'thirty bob' per edition, was very popular at the time and climbed to Book of the Month in the *Evening Standard* Book Awards.

The London taxi trade and the London cabbies are steeped in a long and interesting history. Oliver Cromwell first gave us our charter more than three hundred years ago and Parliament has renewed it without a break over that long period of time. In this book, I will attempt to explain some of the ancient Hackney Carriage Laws that are still on the statute book and try to interpret some of the many vagaries attached to the Conditions of Fitness laid down by the Public Carriage Office (our controlling body) for every licensed taxi in London.

When I did the infamous 'Knowledge of London' over forty years ago, it involved a fourteen thousand-mile slog on a moped around the streets of London, for

God knows how many months. Then, having to answer oral questions on a monthly basis about thousands of streets, hundreds of clubs, theatres, hospitals, etc. to a not-very-nice examiner, before being considered proficient enough to earn the coveted green badge. The class of '61 had to answer those diabolical questions at the old Public Carriage Office in Lambeth Road, which closed in the mid-sixties. The new Public Carriage Office in Penton Street, near the Angel, Islington, introduced some basics such as an appointment system, where the 'Knowledge Boys' were actually given a card with the time and date of their next appointment written on it. This was clearly a major step forward for the nervous youngsters and one we would have dearly welcomed at Lambeth Road. But I can only write about my own experiences; and even streetwise cabbies who have been on the road since the late sixties may find my hair-raising stories about Lambeth Road quite entertaining.

Many of the funny – and sometimes naughty – stories told in this book are from my many friends and acquaintances in the trade, and I devote a whole chapter to the 'girls on the game', the call-girls and the Soho villains. This is not an attempt to titillate my readers. This was London life in the early sixties before the law banning prostitution started taking effect. I also spend a lot of time talking about those weird and wonderful characters who were regular cab 'riders' in those far off days.

London cabbies make up a wide cross-section of society. They come in all shapes and sizes and all colours and, since the Sex Discrimination Act was introduced, they now come in the female form too. We have in our midst ex-professors, former senior police officers, teachers, ex-professional footballers and boxers and a wide range of other callings. From what I can make out from talking to these different people, they originally did the Knowledge only to subsidise their income. Then they got to like the freedom of the job and went full-time cabbing.

I have thoroughly enjoyed my forty years of being a London cabbie and have been lucky enough to indulge my passion for writing as a hobby. My ugly mug has been staring out of the trade papers at the unfortunate cabbies for over thirty years. I have written literally hundreds of articles over that time and also edited a trade magazine for quite a few years. Everybody in the trade knows me as 'Alf the Pipe'. So, to all my many friends and acquaintances in the trade, this is an opportunity for your relatives and friends to read about your job and your life; who knows, you might even be in the book! As licensed taxi-drivers we know what's happening out there on the streets of London. Hopefully, my book will go some way in enabling the ordinary person to appreciate the finest taxi service in the world!

Incidentally, the cabbies' names used in this book are not their real names; in fact they are a compilation of many cabbies. I just wanted to mention that in case I get a 'right-hander'!

ONE

THE KNOWLEDGE

BEFORE THE KNOWLEDGE

Just contemplating doing the Knowledge in 1960 was a pretty daunting prospect for someone in my circumstances at that time. I had no job and I was on remand, accused of a serious criminal charge. We had one child with a second on the way. I had no savings to talk about, so I needed to find a suitable job that would give me some spare time to roam the streets of London for a year or more. I already had a HGV (Heavy Goods Vehicle) licence, so I decided to train for a PSV, which would enable me to drive a coach. Back in those days you didn't get any help or assistance from any of the coach companies; sure, if you held a PSV licence (Passenger Service Vehicle), they would give you a job. But, as for passing the test, you were on your own and had to pay the going rate to hire a coach on the day of your test. With the benefit of hindsight and a huge slice of luck, my choice of date to pass my PSV licence proved to be valuable to me. The little Welsh examiner who passed me for my PSV licence happened to be the very same person who took me on my taxi-driving test a year or so later. I can distinctly remember him saying to me that he knew my face and had I failed the taxi test before? When I told him glibly he had passed me to drive a forty-nine-seater coach a year or so ago, I knew I was home and dry. The failure rate on the taxi-driving test, or 'The Drive' as the boys called it, was quite high. Word had it that some of the examiners took great delight in 'holding back' the Knowledge Boys for one last time before they finally got their coveted green badge. But I knew I was different. The little Welsh examiner couldn't possibly fail my driving on a four-seater taxi when he had already passed me to drive a forty-nine-seater coach! He knew it and he knew that I knew it. When we eventually got back to Lambeth Road in the taxi, the little Welsh examiner – almost grudgingly – told me I had passed my test. But I was very heavy on the clutch – just like a coach driver!

Plan A had succeeded: I had my PSV licence; now I needed a job. Grey-Green Coaches of Stamford Hill was my next stop and I was taken on. The new drivers always got the dodgy jobs where there was no 'beer money', like the school run, the service routes and the changeovers. The changeovers consisted of driving the coach on a service run, stopping at all the stops as far as Brentwood, in Essex. Then on to Colchester, where you would change over with a driver who had come from Great Yarmouth. He would go back whence he came with your coach and you would do the same, with no 'beer money'. I realised much later, when I was a lot wiser, that it was all about 'bunging' the foreman who gave out the work. The same drivers always seemed to get the cream jobs, like the pub outings and trips to the races with the Licensed Victuallers. A coach driver in those days could more than double his weekly wage in tips with trips like these. I really enjoyed the pub outings and the factory outings to dear old Southend. Again, it was a learning curve in life. When you took a crowd of women from a factory in the East End, you needed to be on your best behaviour. They were all out for a good time, but there was a moral limit to their larking about. And if you took a liberty, as in the case of a fellow young driver, you could find yourself minus your trousers and tarred and feathered in the nether regions to boot! I used to give a song in the local pubs at that time, so I was always popular with the ladies and got good 'beer money'.

There was one particular job that nobody wanted to do, so it was given out as a punishment and that eventually meant me. I had left behind a young, unaccompanied mental patient at Colchester coach station. Nobody had told me about this young girl, but the management passed the buck to me. So, I was given the dreaded 'Ghost-Train Run' as my punishment. The Ghost-Train was the very last coach to leave Kings Cross at night, I think it was 10 o'clock. It swept up all the late travellers at every stop as far as Colchester. Then on to Felixstowe and back to Ipswich Garage, which we shared with the Ipswich taxi-drivers. A few hours' kip on the back seat with a blanket, a wake-up call and a cup of tea from the cabbies and it was back heading home to London at 1 minute to 6.

Strangely enough, this job that nobody wanted suited me fine as a potential Knowledge Boy. I could do my runs on my moped for the rest of the morning and early afternoon, then go home and have a sleep before doing the Ghost-Train at night. So, much to the surprise of my fellow drivers, I offered to do the Ghost-Train on a regular basis!

SIGNING ON

In those far-off bureaucratic days, even trying to sign up to do the Knowledge was a pain. The applicant had to produce a photo and a full list of convictions, both criminal and civil. I got in their bad books straight away by forgetting to put down a 'major crime' I had committed as an evacuee in Cornwall during the war. I had been fined a pound by a Magistrate in Newquay for stealing, or 'scrumping', apples.

The situation turned decidedly dodgy, however, when I informed them that I was presently on remand accused of robbery and receiving! The boss of the Public Carriage Office (PCO) called me into his office and told me in no uncertain terms that I could come back if I was found not guilty, but if I was convicted not to bother ever again. Thankfully, the charge was thrown out of court and I went back to my employers to collect three months' back pay that was owing to me. Then I immediately put in my notice, because I knew I was top of the list for being 'fitted up', and applied to the PCO once more. My only claim to fame as a villain was being thrown into a holding cell at Old Street Magistrates Court with the notorious Kray twins, Ronnie and Reggie. I got on all right with the twins because we had mutual friends.

Even as early as the late fifties, the Kray twins had attained a formidable reputation among the London tearaways. Their following swelled, and the Kray myth and the hero-worship began, after they 'defeated' the British Army with their total disobedience of National Service rules and regulations. Despite spending most of their service in the 'glasshouse' (Army prison), they refused to bow to Army discipline. And, speaking from a little experience, that took some doing, because some of those Redcaps in the nick were tough cookies. The Army finally surrendered and got rid of them by giving them a 'DD', a Dishonourable Discharge.

But unless you knew the Krays they didn't look at all like your average villains. Even in the holding cell they were wearing expensive, matching suits, with the square-cut box jackets that exaggerated their barrel chests. Smart silk shirts, matching ties and expensive black leather shoes completed their attire. I can always remember their hair, thick and black and brushed back without a parting. And their prominent black eyebrows seemed to make their eyes even colder and more intimidating.

Luckily for me, we had a mutual friend, and after I had shown my respect for them with the accepted friendly greeting of 'You all right, Ron, you all right, Reg?', I said, 'I'm a mate of Big Patsy out of the Angel.' I received a long, hard stare from those cold eyes. Oh my Gawd, I thought, do they think I'm a police plant? Then Reggie said, 'How's old Patsy doing, is he all right?'

I nodded my reply and the conversation was over as they moved into the corner to discuss some private business. I didn't dare ask them why they were banged-up. But I had heard a whisper on the grapevine that they had been charged with assault with a deadly weapon – after they allegedly cut up a geezer with a bayonet! Incidentally, I heard a few days later that the twins had walked free from the alleged bayonet attack. And why? Simple – nobody had the bottle to give evidence against them. And I made them right if they wanted to carry on living!

What always fascinated and intrigued me many years later, after the Krays had built up a criminal empire, was why they got involved personally with the murder and violence that got them locked away for the rest of their lives? They had many underlings to do their dirty work. So was it simply a macho thing to show all and sundry who was still boss?

As for me, on the day, I was treated like royalty in the holding cell, because the old custody sergeant wrongly believed I was one of the firm. He kept calling me 'mate' and asking me if I wanted another cup of tea or a fag and was I all right.

When my name was called to walk up the steps to the dock, I don't mind telling you I nearly wet myself with fright. Take it from me, it's one of the scariest – and loneliest – things in life. You suddenly surface from the dark depths of the cell area, into the bright lights of the courtroom and a hubbub of noise. And there, looking down on me, was this skeletal face wearing those funny specs with half-frames. This was the 'Beak', or Magistrate, and sitting next to him was a rather large lady with freshly-permed hair and big, muscular arms. I remember thinking at the time – I always think funny things when I'm stressed – that she would be better suited with a whistle in her mouth and blowing it for the bully-off in a 'gels' hockey match!

I had been well versed by my legal team and I stuck to my story religiously, trying all the time to look innocent, even though with my muscular frame and broken nose, I looked a bigger villain than the Krays! But the turning point of my trial really came when the prosecution called in their star witness. He was a real old carrot-cruncher that they had pulled in from way out in the sticks. You could tell from the off that he was wetting himself more than me – and he wasn't even on trial! The odds were that he'd never left his Suffolk village before, let alone appeared in a London courtroom. I saw the look of utter despair on the top cop's face as my barrister tore the old guy to pieces. It appeared that the old guy was in charge of a bonded warehouse. Now, for the uninitiated, a bonded warehouse is only ever opened on clearance by HM Customs, and the prosecution's entire case rested on the fact that I had been arrested for having stolen property in my house in August. Yet the bonded warehouse holding that property hadn't been cleared by Customs until the following month. This proved, without a doubt, that the goods had been stolen at my depot, while in transit to the warehouse, by a person or persons unknown. Yet my smart-arsed barrister persuaded this old carrot-cruncher to tell the court that, yes, it could have been possible for someone to have stolen some of the contents of the bonded warehouse and sold them on to me, without his knowledge, of course.

For sure, I was elated when the Beak threw the case out, much to the chagrin of the top cop, who had spent months collecting the evidence. But I had a guilty conscience about the old guy who had been given a roasting for being so naive and honest. And more than four decades down the line, I still feel guilty – especially when they had me bang to rights. So, instead of going down for a long stretch, as the 'friendly' top cop had previously told my wife, I walked out into the spring sunshine a free man.

Sadly, many of my good mates at the time got themselves involved in criminal activities and finished up doing time. But not me. I make no bones about it, I had been extremely fortunate to walk away scot-free. But that experience had frightened the living daylights out of me and has been indelibly imprinted in my mind for more than forty years. So, a couple of years down the line, after I had managed to complete the dreaded Knowledge of London and gained the coveted Green Badge, I vowed, for the sake of my wife and kids, that I would never leave the straight and narrow again. I had scrimped and saved and worked like a dog to get that Green Badge and there was no way I was going to lose it by getting involved in shady deals, or buying 'bent' gear. And, touch wood, all these years later I've kept to my promise. Mind you, I'm not quite as straight as your Roman roads!

THE INTERVIEW

My record had been checked, I had no County Court summonses pending, the photo really was of me, so it was interview time for the Knowledge. All the new boys were ushered into a bare room at Lambeth Road, a crumbling Edwardian edifice that seemed more like a prison. We waited in awe for the Chief Examiner. In those far-off days, all the staff and examiners were ex-policemen, so immediately, they didn't like taxi-drivers or even potential taxi-drivers. Their attitude could best be termed as disdainful, or at worst, totally bored and unhelpful. After many months on the course, I realised that their rudeness and disdain were a deliberate ploy to make you lose your temper, a bit like the drill sergeant in the Army. Once they got you wound up and you blew your top, that was the end. You were no longer deemed to be 'a fit and proper person to become a licensed taxi-driver' and you were thrown off the course – permanently.

The Chief Examiner entered the room surrounded by his assistants, almost like royalty as I recall. He was a wiry little guy in a smart suit and his grey-flecked hair was swept back tight on his head and plastered down with Brylcreem. He sported a neatly-clipped Hitler-type moustache. But the thing that impressed me the most was his ramrod-straight back. It was so straight and rigid, almost as though he was wearing a corset! He moved in a whippet-like way and his eyes were looking all over the class. With my recent unpleasant experience of National Service, I immediately said under my breath, 'This guy's just gotta be ex-military, probably a long-serving Colour Sergeant or even a Regimental Sergeant Major.' Yes, I could well see him on the parade ground, patiently measuring out the paces with his stick!

He stopped at the top table and his minions lined up either side of him, whilst we all looked on nervously. He was obviously enjoying every minute of being the focal point, almost like reliving his military past and giving a briefing to the SAS or a crack commando unit before a daring raid. I remember thinking to myself at the time, this guy likes the sound of his own voice and I'll lay a hundred pounds to a penny, that he calls us 'laddie'. And I was spot on! He cast a beady eye around the room attempting to get some eye contact. 'Has anyone tried this before?' he asked in a thin, reedy voice. Everyone looked round when a couple of the guys put their hands up rather timidly. 'Well I never,' he chuckled, 'I reckon you two blokes must be barking mad.' His assistants started chuckling, so I started chuckling, just a little too heartily. He fixed his beady eyes on me and, walking across, he shouted, 'It's not that funny, laddie, because doing the Knowledge just once can drive you mad. So, if these two gents are starting it for the second time, they must be barking mad.'

Right, I thought to myself, it's just like National Service and the drill sergeants. Keep your head down and don't get noticed. After the initial jokey start, it was down to business and the distribution of the 'Blue Book', containing over four hundred runs or routes that criss-crossed all over London. Up piped the reedy voice again. Holding a white pamphlet up in his outstretched hand, he said theatrically, 'This white pamphlet that I am a-holding up for all of you to peruse is called, believe it or not, the "Blue Book". Some of you may be thinking, why is it called the "Blue Book" when it's white?' Then chuckling to himself at his own clever humour, he continued: 'You may think that I am so clever I will know the answer. But I don't. It was called that by taxi-drivers many years ago and nobody knows why.'

Again, a ripple of laughter from his audience while he stood beaming, holding his thumbs in his waistcoat. 'This "Blue Book" is your Bible,' he went on. 'You need to learn every single run by heart. And you need to be able to recite each and every one of the four hundred runs and be able to see all the streets in your head.' He paused to make sure there was fear in all of our eyes, then he continued in full flow, 'As if that's not enough, you will need to learn all the many hundreds of points of interest that you pass on every run and be able to spot the run when the starting and finishing points are changed by your examiner during your monthly tests.' He grinned to himself, while a murmur of disbelief came from his captive audience. 'We're wise to all the tricks up here,' he went on. 'If we were only to ask you simple points like Piccadilly or Buckingham Palace, you'd all be sitting at home on your backsides, just map-reading, wouldn't you, eh?' He cast a beady eye on his shell-shocked audience, just to make sure his comments had been digested, before going on again: 'Let me warn you gentlemen,' he said in a sombre voice, 'if any of my examiners inform me that they think one of you is sitting on his arse map-reading at home, you'll be in for the high jump. We caught one joker last week who was calling over a run and he decided to turn right from Holborn Viaduct into Farringdon Street, which is a fifty foot drop to the street below.'

He paused to receive his expected applause, his men were laughing and the joke was obviously an 'old chestnut'. Many of us didn't know where the hell Holborn Viaduct was, but we still had to force a laugh – it seemed to be expected. The Chief Examiner started gathering up his papers and looking around the room, almost as though he was looking for a face he didn't like. I kept my head buried in the Blue Book, looking as studious as possible. 'Right, gentlemen,' he said, standing up, 'the rest is up to you. If you want to become a London taxi-driver, you will need to work very hard at it, day and night.' He started towards the door followed by his entourage, and with a last theatrical gesture he turned and said, 'I want you all back here in fifty-six days, bright and early and ready to answer any question about London. Keep at it, lads.'

Then he was gone. That was it, you were on your own. No advice about the best way to do the runs or learn the points. No advice about the length of time to spend on each run. In fact, no advice on anything remotely connected to the Knowledge. We had been issued with our Blue Books and been forced to listen to his monthly waffle. Now it was time to put up, or shut up. Many of our class of '61 wouldn't make it – the drop-out rate was around 70 per cent. But I was determined, I would never give up – nor would my as-yet unborn son, thirty years later.

MANOR HOUSE TO GIBSON SQUARE

All the twenty-odd thousand London cabbies, plus the many, many thousands of hopefuls who failed to complete the Knowledge, will recognise that 'Manor House to Gibson Square' is the start of your penance. This is the very first run, on the very first page of your Blue Book. How you face this run and how you learn it will determine your success or failure doing the other 400-odd runs. If your original gameplan was to go from A to B in the quickest possible time, then do all the rest of the runs in a similar manner, you'll be in for a big shock, my friends!

The secret of holding all the information in your

brain is to do just three runs every day, but to make sure you do them properly. Cruise around within a quarter of a mile or so of the starting point, jotting down the names of all the buildings, like hospitals, police stations, theatres and just about everything else. Do exactly the same when you are on the run, put them all down in your book. At the finishing point, repeat what you did at the start of the run.

Back in the early sixties, there was only one Knowledge School. That was opposite the Oval Cricket Ground and run by the British Legion for ex-servicemen. My two years of National Service in the RAF certainly didn't open any doors for me! It's a lot different today, because I'm told it's quite a lucrative business and the Knowledge Boys have a wide choice of schools. You pay your fee, you get a full printed list of the up-to-date runs and the latest 'points' asked by the different examiners. And you can attend a class at any given time and practise 'call-overs' with the tutor and the rest of the class. Not so, back in the early sixties. A large wall map was required, with two pins and a length of cotton. All the old-timers used to tell me to 'keep to the cotton' for the straightest run. So, the evening before you started, you stuck a pin in Manor House, tied on the cotton and stretched it in a straight line as far as Gibson Square. Then you copied out all of the route on 'the cotton'. This you would have to do over four hundred times before completing the Blue Book. This method may sound slightly quaint, or even antiquated by today's high-tech ways of doing it. But, surprisingly enough, it was highly effective because you learned the 'cotton' route by copying it into your book, then you did the run on your bike. Finally, you copied the completed run into your best book, ready for call-overs. In effect, you actually learned it twice as many times, compared to today's method of having runs ready-printed.

The winters in London seemed a lot, lot colder forty years ago and I was absolutely freezing on my little scooter. I can't remember any quality waterproof gear around at that time, and even if there had been, I wouldn't have been able to afford to buy it. So, my dear wife used to tie black plastic dustbin liners around my legs and an old balaclava on my head before I ventured out on the Knowledge. I must have looked like a cross between a rag and bone man and a bank robber.

But I persisted, I had to for the sake of my wife and child. I would put the coach in the garage in the mornings, get on my scooter, do my three runs every day and sleep in the afternoon, before picking up the coach again for the Ghost-Train. Driving up to Felixstowe in the dark, I would call over the runs in my head I had learned that day: 'Leave on the left Piccadilly, left Half Moon Street, left into Curzon Street, right into South Audley Street, left into Mount Street, right into Park Street, cross Oxford Street into Portman Street, forward into Gloucester Place' and so on and so on, all the way to Swiss Cottage.

But time was pushing by and suddenly the fifty-six days were up and I had to brush up all my knowledge for my very first 'appearance'. Thanks to my wife checking my regular call-overs every day, I was reasonably confident of answering. But how wrong can one be? If you think about it, I had learned by heart some thirty or forty runs, but the examiner could ask me questions on any of the four hundred runs. I'm really glad I didn't consider that option at the time.

MY FIRST APPEARANCE

One would have thought that since the Public Carriage Office in Lambeth Road was a government building, and had catered for hundreds of hopeful 'Knowledge Boys' every year since 1927, they would have installed a tried-and-tested system. Not a bit of it. There was no appointment system, there was not even a recognised system of simply asking the boys back in alphabetical order, and it was left to the boys themselves to sort out who they followed into the examiner. For the full ten months it took me to get my badge, all I can recall is being known in a loud voice as 'Next'.

So it was up bright and early on a freezing winter's morning – a friend of mine had told me it was best to get there early and not risk losing a day. Out with the battered scooter, and wearing about four layers of vests, football shirts and a sweater, off I pop-popped to Lambeth Road. My heart sank when I pulled up outside the PCO. It was only about 7.30 a.m., yet there were already a dozen or so blokes queuing up on the steps outside. They were dressed in an assortment of cold-weather gear, ranging from bright yellow fishermen's outfits, to Russian-style fur hats and ski boots, and all deeply engrossed in studying maps and atlases. The young fella at the back of the queue turned around to me and said, 'You follow me, mate. Stick your scooter outside the caff, get a couple of "rosie leas" and I'll keep your place for you.'

So that was the system the old hands operated. I get him a tea, he saves my place and I do the same for the next guy. I reckon we stood outside that crumbling, Edwardian edifice for the best part of two hours in the freezing cold and rain. Suddenly, there was the sound of bolts being slid back, then the creaking of the big, old-fashioned door as it was pulled open and a wag at the back brought a ripple of nervous laughter as he said in a deep dark-brown voice, just like the late actor Valentine Dyall, playing the Man in Black, 'Well-l-l-come to Dra-cula's Castle.'

We all shuffled in, happy to be out of the cold, and I just followed all those who knew the ropes. I peeked through the glass-panelled, cold, austere offices we passed and the men I noticed inside looked as cold and austere as their surroundings. These were obviously the dreaded examiners, because on the tops of their desks were large, upright boards, with street maps of London tacked on. When your time came to face 'the firing squad', they could see you, but all you saw was the top of a head. We all clattered down, would you believe, an ancient, cast-iron spiral staircase, to the lower ground floor and our 'home' for many months, the dreaded 'Dungeon', or 'Snake-Pit'.

London cabbies from my era will still remember the dreaded Snake-Pit as a lingering nightmare. Obviously converted from an old, filthy, disused office, or even a large holding cell for Edwardian baddies, the room was below ground level, and apart from a weak, bare bulb the only other semblance of light came through the grimy, stained window at street level, just enabling you to see a pair of shoes walking past on a bright, sunny day. I suppose you could describe the decor as shiny Edwardian puce, cleverly mixed with a half century of smog and grime! Someone had thought to place a dozen forms across the room for the 'cons' to sit on. But the *pièce de resistance* of this 'bijou residence' was the stinking toilet in the corner. I noticed all the regulars were sitting 'up wind' and well away from 'Thomas Crapper's Mark One Model'!

Being British, we tend to hold back when talking about toilets or daily bodily functions. But this particular toilet needs talking about. You have to remember there were about thirty guys down there, all nervously reading their runs and maps, feeling a bit gyppy in their tummies and some suffering from claustrophobia. So when the call eventually came down the spiral stairs, 'Who's first?', the bodily juices really started to flow and a queue soon formed outside the toilet. The tragedy was that these poor guys didn't have any privacy, everybody could loudly hear their problems. And you don't need that when you're being physically sick. As for me, I was six or seven years older than these kids. I had done my National Service in the RAF and seen it all before. Besides, I had a family to worry about.

The shaky nerves, the gyppy tummies and the reek of the foul-smelling toilet continued all the morning, broken every half hour or so by one of the Knowledge Boys coming out from his exam and shouting down the spiral staircase, 'Next!' Then, round about 1 o'clock, another, more authoritative voice shouted down, 'All right, the rest of you lads down there, buzz off and get yourself some grub for an hour.'

Then it was a quick dash next door to Marcantonio's café and a nice, steaming hot mug of tea and a bacon sandwich. It was also the opportunity to chat to some of the boys who had already been in the firing line, and were still hanging around waiting for their mates. They started telling us what points and what runs the examiner had thrown at them. Along with many of the others, I suddenly got into a blind panic. Where on earth were Apsley House, the Reform Club and the In and Out Club? Where the hell were the Churchill Clinic, the London Clinic, or the Marie Curie Clinic? The list of runs came tumbling out, but if you didn't know the point, you couldn't start the run. This was getting a bit like brain damage to me and I decided to concentrate on what I'd been learning and just hope he asked me some of those. So we all filed back in, well before the hour was up and sat around with our maps and books on our laps, desperately trying to concentrate. I suppose it was around 3 o'clock and I had just two blokes in front of me, when the authoritative voice suddenly shouted down again, 'That's the lot for today. Put your names in the book when you come up and you'll be first on the list if you can make it tomorrow.'

And that was that. I had lost a night's work, I had come out early in the freezing cold and queued up on those windswept steps for God knows how long, had suffered violent stomach pains through nerves and stress and I'd felt sick and unwell because of that stinking toilet. And what did I get for my eight hours of purgatory? 'That's the lot for today.'

I was absolutely fuming by the time I reached the top of the spiral staircase and my hand was trembling with rage as I signed my name in the book. I very nearly blew it before I had even started. It was only the sound of a friendly voice talking to me that saved the day. 'Are you all right, lad?' said this elderly chap with grey hair. 'You look a bit peaky.' I took in a deep breath, thought about my wife and baby relying on me, and wiping my brow, I managed to mutter, 'Oh, I'm all right, sir, I'm just feeling a bit giddy with the lack of fresh air.' 'Is this your first appearance, lad?' inquired the grey-haired guy. I nodded in reply and carried on wiping my brow, trying very hard not to show my anger. 'I thought as much,' he replied, 'the first time is always the worst.' He looked at my name on the list and said, 'You come and see me tomorrow, Mr Townsend, and we'll see if we can't make you a good cabbie.'

Without that kindly and sympathetic intervention, I know full well that I would have blown my top in frustration and been slung off the course forever. That was the first – and the very last – bit of sympathy I ever received from the examiners!

Ask any London cabbie what was the very first question they were asked on the Knowledge and they will surely remember it. It's a bit like your service number in the forces, or even your Mum's number with the Co-op. I started the next day exactly like the previous one, only this time around, I was the very first up the spiral stairs. The kindly, grey-haired chap was seated behind his desk and he gave me a pleasant 'Good morning' and asked me to sit down. 'So, have you been hard at it, Mr Townsend?' he asked. I explained my circumstances and informed him I had been doing three runs a day for two months.

'Yes, that's ample,' he replied, leaning back in his chair. 'Right then, let's try you out. Take me from Bowling Green Lane to Bowling Green Alley.' That was my very first question and I didn't know it, and I didn't know the next five questions either. In fact, all I said was, 'Sorry, sir, I don't know that one.' So, it was back again in fifty-six days!

Something rather strange happened towards the end of the next fifty-six days. In cab parlance it was known as 'holding it', as opposed to 'dropping it'. The vast amounts of knowledge that my brain was accumulating suddenly started to register in sequence and I could shut my eyes and actually see the colour of the doors at some of the gentlemen's clubs in Pall Mall. The Knowledge itself is basically a process of elimination, almost like a giant jigsaw puzzle and the workrate involved is comparable to a three-year university degree. So, the further you ploughed your way through the Blue Book, doing external call-overs every evening of course, the more your brain tuned in like a modern computer, then stored everything on file.

But, unfortunately, with possible questions being asked on more than four hundred runs, it was obvious that the process of elimination would take quite a few months. And so it proved with me. I didn't answer a single question on my second appearance, or a single question on my third appearance. So, in effect, I had been beavering away on the Knowledge for around six hard months and all I had come up with was, 'I'm sorry, sir, I'm afraid I don't know that one!' Nowadays I believe you don't get an appearance until you've completed the Blue Book, about a year I think. This helps to streamline the Knowledge and cuts out much of the wasted time of boys like me saying, 'I'm sorry, sir, I haven't done that run yet.'

Strangely enough, I was quite happy and confident. I had known the runs on my three appearances, but couldn't remember the points to start me off. Around that time, I happened to have a little win on the football pools, so I decided to have a break, take the family to Malta and blow the money. As bad luck would have it, while we were away sunning ourselves, the Earls Court one-way system was opened. I just knew that questions on the new one-way system would be top of the examiner's list and I knew I needed to check it out before my next appearance. But I didn't. My dear wife convinced me it wasn't the end of the world, but it almost was for me. As I suspected, half of the questions were about the new one-way system. I told the examiner I had been away on holiday, he was unusually sympathetic, but I managed to guess a couple and I answered all the others. He actually said to me, 'Well done, lad' and I had a sneaking feeling I was on my way. My fifth appearance was pure magic. A full house, every question spot on, after which the examiner said the magic words, 'I'm going to give you a reduction, lad. You've been working hard, so come back in twenty-eight days.'

All the hard work had been worth it. Once you got your reduction, you were on your way, but still needing to graft hard. Both of my 28s were highly successful and suddenly I was on my 21s and my 14s. Then he said, 'Come back in seven days.' Finally, it was down to doing the suburbs by map-reading. Many of the guys found the suburbs very difficult and some of them took three months or more to hack it. But not an old coach driver like me. I used my London knowledge to take me to the North or South Circular and just buzzed around them to places like Cheam, Sutton, Edmonton, Crystal Palace and Croydon. The examiner noticed it as well, saying, 'You must be a coach or lorry driver, laddie!'

By this time I had signed up with a cab garage to borrow a taxi to practise my 'wangling'. Now don't ask me where this expression came from. All I know is that you borrowed a taxi to practise your driving and took it up for your test or 'drive'. In return, you signed a contract to do three months' night work for that garage. Anyway, that's what the procedure was forty years ago.

As I stated at the start of the chapter, I was lucky enough on my drive to get the very same examiner who passed me for my PSV licence to drive a coach. So we did the three-point turn in a narrow little street off Hercules Road, called Carlisle Lane. And, when I say narrow, I mean narrow. I reckon with the cab in the centre of the lane, only a couple of feet front and back were left to manoeuvre. This is where many of the examiners used to crucify the nervous Knowledge Boys. Then we had a very pleasant ride around the West End, while he picked up some Christmas presents for his wife and family.

So, finally, back to the suburbs. I had made one appearance and was asked to return for a second. Imagine my utter surprise and delight the following day when, after rattling off a couple of questions, still using the North and South Circulars, the examiner said to me, with a genuine smile on his face, 'I think that will do, lad. Go out to the office while I complete this form. When that's done, you can come and collect your badge.'

That sentence was like music to my ears. It was coming up to Christmas and I had been pounding the streets of London in the day and driving up to Felixstowe five nights a week, for almost ten months. Now it was finished – I was a fully-fledged, London cabbie and issued with my brand-new, shiny badge, number 5642. I've still got the same badge, but not as shiny!

Now for the ritual in Marcantonio's café next door, and it was time for the other boys to feel envious. I had sat in that café for what seemed like an eternity, watching the guys come in and proudly show off their shiny new badges. Now it was my moment of triumph. I went over to my little gang at first and showed them my trophy. Two of them had already failed their drive and the other two were to take another three months to complete their suburbs. But they were pleased for me. We had spent many, many hours on the road together, some happy and some, not so happy. Especially the time when we were doing the run to Kensal Green Cemetery and sitting in the café opposite having a hot cup of tea. We had parked our scooters outside so that we could keep an eye on them and were casually watching this lorry backing in. It backed and continued to back, and suddenly we all realised that it wasn't going to stop before hitting our precious scooters. So we all rushed out shouting, 'Stop, stop, you're gonna whack our scooters.'

But to no avail. The driver just carried on backing and finished up mangling our scooters! Then this old boy gets out of the lorry, wearing thick Tizer-bottle glasses, totally ignorant of the mayhem he'd caused. But we took pity on him because he said he'd 'ave lost his job if the guv'nor found out he had dodgy minces (mince-pies, eyes). So he ran us all home and we claimed on the insurance, even though it kept us off the road for a while.

I savoured the moment of glory. The guys were all crowding round looking lovingly at my shiny new badge. The tea was flowing like wine and even the guv'nor came over to wish me luck. His luck didn't last too long, because when the old PCO moved a few years later, the café went skint and closed down.

I eventually left the café and the feeling was quite strange. We had all lived in one another's pockets for the past ten months and the cameraderie among the lads was great. We used to have a whip-round for any of the guys off sick. We helped each other with runs and with points and tried to work as a team. No matter whether you were rich or poor, we were all in it together. In those days, I reckon the London Cab Trade was about sixty, or even seventy per cent Jewish. You could always tell the Jewish guys in their expensive ski jackets and great big fur boots. I believe a lot of them were subsidised by their dads, many of them already cabmen. But I got on well with most of them and we have remained good friends until this day.

Now I was on my own. No more freezing cold scooters. No more call-overs or monthly tests. I had finally cracked it. I made my way proudly across the road to where *my* cab was parked. I drove along Lambeth Road, did a left into Kennington Road and, lo and behold, I trapped my very first fare. 'Please take me to the Cottage Club in Tottenham Court Road,' said the smart gent, jumping in.

Absolute blind panic gripped me. I had learned every road, every street and every club in London for the past ten months. But where the hell was the Cottage Club? I didn't know it then, and forty years on, I still don't know it! But the punter didn't mind. I dropped him half-way up Tottenham Court

Road, just by the old Continental Cinema and told him that I had just passed out on the Knowledge and it was customary for a Knowledge Boy to give his very first fare a free ride. I think it's supposed to bring you luck for the rest of your career, or so the old timers used to tell us.

The following morning I awoke with great excitement and, looking out of my bedroom window, I could see *my* cab parked by the kerb. The first thing I needed to do was to go up to Stamford Hill and collect my employment cards from Grey-Green Coaches. All the other coach-drivers gathered around my cab, all taking the mickey out of me and calling me by my garage nickname of 'Manningtree'. This unfortunate nickname came about when I had to cut through from Felixstowe to Harwich late one night in an empty coach. The guys had already warned me about the low bridge at Manningtree and to make certain the sunroof was closed on top. It was late and I was tired, but the loud scraping noise I heard when going under the low bridge soon woke me up. I forced the sunroof shut and continued nervously on my way.

The next day I dumped the coach in the garage and made a speedy exit without telling anyone. It didn't take the garage too long to trace the driver and I was up in front of the big boss yet again. Old George Ewer was all right, very much the English gent, and he wouldn't even allow a union in his garage. He suspended me from driving coaches for a month and I became his personal chauffeur, driving his brand-new Jaguar up and down the A12 to Colchester and back.

I said my fond farewells to all my fellow drivers and pulled out into the main road. I hadn't gone a hundred yards when I was hailed by a couple of 'froomers', that's Jewish slang for the Orthodox Jews who wear the big beards. They asked me if I would be interested in taking them around North London for a couple of hours. Now you have to remember, I was a total novice and had no idea of how to price a job for two hours. So I just nodded and put the meter on. I think they must have been property owners and were calling round for the rents. We went to places like Enfield, Edmonton, Chingford, Walthamstow and Stoke Newington, then back again. The job was probably worth twice as much, but when we arrived back after four hours, I had a massive amount of money on the meter and they gave me a couple of quid on top as well. They knew they had had a blinding 'result' with a new boy, but I was tickled pink. Okay, I realised I had to pay forty per cent of the meter takings to my guv'nor, but that still left me with more than the week's wages I had been previously earning on the coaches, after doing just one fare in the cab. After all the scrimping and saving for a whole year, I felt like a millionaire. This cabbing will suit me fine, I thought. I was old enough and wise enough to realise that it wouldn't be sunshine every day on the cab. But at least I'd always be able to provide for my wife and family.

TWO

FROM HORSES TO HORSELESS CARRIAGES

Quoting from the book, *The History Of The Cab Trade*, written by my dear friend and cab trade historian, Philip Warren, enables me to give you some insight into the speedy transition from horses to horseless carriages in London. He writes:

The Hansom cab and the 'growler', or to give it its correct name, the 'Clarence' were to reign supreme in the London cab trade until they were ousted by the internal combustion engine. Before the dawning of that age however, the Hansom was to undergo another change. The man responsible was Henry Forder of the Forder Cab Company, Wolverhampton. His alterations were to make the Hansom cab probably the finest horse-drawn carriage in the world at that time, the cab to which Disraeli referred to as 'The Gondola of London'.

By far the most important of Forder's improvements was the re-introduction of the straight axle. This he achieved by cutting away the body of the cab under the passenger's seat at an angle of forty-five degrees, sloping to the floor where the passenger's feet rested. He also raised the driver's seat so that the cabby sat seven feet off the ground, his weight counterbalanced by the shafts, giving a perfectly balanced vehicle. In addition, as the weight was taken off the horse, it was possible to attain a greater speed which, in certain conditions, could be as high as 17 m.p.h. . . . .

The London cabmen in those days worked under appalling conditions and were expected to sit 'on the box' in rain, snow, cold and wind, waiting for a fare. No wonder many of them found solace from the foul weather by nipping into the grog shop, fortifying themselves with mugs of hot cocoa with a nip of rum. 'In January 1875', writes Philip Warren, 'a Captain J. Armstrong, Editor of the *Globe* newspaper and who lived in St John's Wood, sent his manservant out into a blizzard that was raging at the time, to engage a cab to take Captain Armstrong to his office in Fleet St. Returning a full hour later with a cab, the Captain enquired of his servant why he had been so long. He was told that although the cabs were on the rank, the cabmen had retired to a nearby grog shop to get out of the blizzard'.

Captain Armstrong spoke to many of his friends about the fact that cabmen had nowhere to shelter from the elements. They all sympathised with the cabmen and decided to donate money for the erection of a shelter adjacent to the cab rank in Acacia Road, St John's Wood – and so was born the London Cabmen's Shelter Fund. Many wealthy and influential people including the Prince of Wales, and later as King Edward VII, subscribed to the fund. One shelter, erected in Old Palace Yard, Westminster, was paid for by Members of both Houses of Parliament, the list of subscribers reading like a page from Debrett's Peerage.

At first, the shelters had no provision for supplying meals – but by 1882 larger shelters were erected, which included a small kitchen and hot meals and drinks were provided by the shelter keeper. Many of the shelters in Central London were frequented late at night by well-known personalities, who would pop in for a cup of steaming hot cocoa and a slice of 'Tottenham'. Sir Ernest Shackleton, the explorer, was a regular visitor to the old shelter which stood at Hyde Park Corner. Prior to his last expedition, where he tragically died at sea, the cabmen who used this shelter presented Shackleton with a set of pipes and a pipe rack. His letter of thanks to them hung there for many years until the shelter was pulled down to make way for the Hyde Park Underpass. Incidentally, in the seventies, a regular visitor at night in the Pont Street shelter was the famous Hollywood movie star and former wife of Frank Sinatra, Ava Gardner. But she was no longer the screen beauty she had been. She looked plump and overweight, possibly owing to a drink problem.

During the next seventy-five years, some forty-seven of these shelters were erected at the larger cab ranks in inner London. But, owing to road changes at places like Marble Arch and Great Portland St, they have since declined to about thirteen in number. But these thirteen remaining shelters have become Grade Two listed buildings and are now refurbished by English Heritage. So they will live on.

THE PCO

The ruling body over all London taxis is the Public Carriage Office. Their history goes back as far as 1662, when they were known as the Hackney Coach Office. 'Before 1885', writes Philip, 'the Public Carriage Office of the Metropolitan Police was located at 4, Whitehall Place. Then, in that year the famous building known the world over as Scotland Yard was built and some 2,500 tons of granite was used in its construction. All this granite was quarried and dressed by prisoners at Dartmoor. Here, the Public Carriage Office remained until 1927, when, as a result of expansion, a new police building was erected at 109 Lambeth Road. In 1966, the Public Carriage Office moved to 15 Penton Street, Islington.'

'Despite the deplorable drop in standards generally in the post-war period, the standard set by 300 years of continual licensing have always been kept. The London cab trade would not have it any other way. The Public Carriage Office is a unique institution and most probably there is no other body in the world quite like it', writes Philip.

I do agree in essence with Philip's thoughts on the PCO, but here's the rub. The world has changed dramatically since Britain had her Empire and many trade organisations and drivers believe the PCO hasn't changed with it. There are many anomalies that the PCO still adheres to and the modern cabbies believe they are insular, undemocratic and in some instances, unlawful. One of the biggest bones of contention with the PCO is their policy of answering complaints from the public. If you were to stop and analyse this policy, it would appear almost feudal to the outsider. What you have to remember is that, firstly, the vast majority of London cabbies are honest and hard-working. As in any other levels of society there are a few black sheep in the flock. But the PCO seem to adopt the attitude that all cabbies are black sheep, until they can prove themselves otherwise. So, in effect, whenever you are called up to answer a written complaint, you have to prove that the letter-writer's complaint is unfounded, and if you can't disprove it – and you have a history of many complaints, even if they are not proven – you could well have your licence revoked.

Any cabbie, who may live many miles away from the PCO, may suddenly receive a letter from them asking him/her to come in and answer the complaint. The complaint may well be trivial, or even spiteful and anti-taxi, but the cabbie is forced to lose half a day's work to clear himself. One driver I know was called in to be told that one of his lady passengers had accused him of 'talking dirty and exposing himself'. That would be difficult to do in a cab at Oxford Circus in the rush hour, and, as it turned out, the woman was a compulsive letter-writer. From day one, and with a little knowledge of the law, I have always refused to attend the PCO to answer a written complaint, unless the complainant attends with their solicitor. Then I would be happy to do likewise.

My resolve stemmed from an incident about twenty years ago. I picked up a pleasant-seeming old gent early one Sunday afternoon at Paddington Station and took him to St James's Court, Buckingham Gate. He paid me off and gave me a decent tip and I drove off. Two weeks later I got the letter from the PCO, telling me to come and answer a complaint for overcharging. So for the very first and only time, I went up to the PCO. It appears that the fare wasn't as pleasant as I had at first thought. He alleged that he did the journey every Saturday and that I had overcharged him by 50p – honestly! So the PCO wanted me to refund the 50p and that would be the end of the matter. But I refused point blank. I explained that if they checked the days of travel stated they would realise that there was a difference of some 20p on the 'extra' charges between a Saturday and Sunday. Also, Constitution Hill is closed on Sundays, which would add a further 20p to the metered fare. I am reliably informed that any complaint, even if it's not proven, goes on your file for future reference. Is that democratic?

Some of the antiquated Hackney Carriage Laws still on the statute book tend to make our historic trade a bit of a laughing stock – especially when it's the 'Silly

Season' and the press can't think of anything sensible to write about. We all know about the need to carry a bale of hay on the cab to feed the horse and we all know that the cabman's right to refuse a fare over six miles was mooted a century ago, so as not to tire the horses. As for it being legal for a cabman to urinate on the nearside rear wheel of his cab with the back door open, well, I wonder if a Magistrate would support an ancient Hackney Carriage Law if the perpetrator was charged with public indecency?

Some of the Conditions of Fitness that every London taxi has to pass to be licensed are rather strange in this modern world. Mind you, I honestly believe the strictness of these conditions has gone a long way in helping to preserve the unique, custom-built taxi that's recognised the world over. Without the famed 25-foot turning circle of the London taxi and the requirement that it has to be high enough to enable a 'gentleman in a top hat' to enter, I am certain the custom-built cab would have disappeared years ago.

Another fascinating part of the PCO is the Lost Property Office in the same building. Every single item found in a London taxi and handed in at police stations all over the Metropolitan Police district is collected a couple of times a week by a little grey van and sorted out at the Lost Property Office. Again, this is unique to the London cab trade and the practice has existed for many years. When the owner is eventually traced, they are charged an administration cost and a small percentage that goes to the driver who found the item. If the item is particularly valuable, like an expensive ring or suchlike, they are asked if they would like to donate something extra to the cabbie. If the item is not claimed by the owner after a period of three months, it goes to the finder, the cabbie. And if he doesn't claim it within three months of handing it in, the proceeds go to the Metropolitan Police Fund.

I wrote an article on the Lost Property Office many years ago and had a very revealing day up there getting some research. You just wouldn't believe the things that some people leave in taxis: boxes of jewellery, sets of golf clubs, valuable paintings and, in one instance, a baby in a pushchair! In the case of money and very valuable items, the Lost Property Office operates a sliding scale of reward. If the amount of money or the value of a ring comes to many hundreds of pounds, then the reward can be as little as a penny per hundred over a certain amount. Many of my cabbie friends who have handed in large amounts of money have told me they think this is unfair. But the bottom line is that it's not your property and if you were to hand in something you'd found on the Underground, or the buses, you'd get nowt!

A classic example occurred not long after my article came out in the trade press. A very dear friend phoned me up and said he'd found a fat wallet in his cab containing about £4,000, and what should he do with it? I advised him to hand it in, or take the chance of 'doing his Bill'. Anyway, he took my advice and a couple of weeks later he phoned me again and said, 'I handed that dough in like you suggested and I feel a lot better for doing it.' 'It just ain't worth the aggro, John,' I said. 'I tell you what mate,' he went on in an excited voice, 'one of the chaps told me I was on ten per cent, so I've booked a nice long weekend in Paris on the strength of it.' I paused for a while to consider what he'd said and started working out what I thought he'd get as a reward, using the sliding scale I'd recently learned from the Lost Property Office. I had to tell him the facts, even though he'd be disappointed. 'You really shouldn't listen to these blokes in the shelters, John,' I said, 'I've worked it out and you'll be lucky to get a day in Brighton with your reward, 'cos I reckon you'll cop about £29.70.'

A few weeks went by and John phoned again and I knew he was feeling a bit sheepish, because he'd pooh-poohed the estimated sum I'd originally given him, and I was only 30p out! 'You were right, mate, and the geezers in the shelter were wrong,' he said. 'Mind you, I did cop thirty pence more than you estimated.'

In the vast majority of cases, the Lost Property Office's tried and trusted system works adequately. But, over the years, I have heard rumblings of discontent and accusations of alleged skulduggery along the line. For instance, many years ago a very dear friend of mine purchased a length of expensive mohair cloth, to have a suit made up. I believe this cloth had 'fallen off the back of a lorry'! Anyway, he was driving home late one night in his cab and got pulled over at a police road block. They immediately spotted the roll of cloth standing upright in the luggage section, and asked him where he had obtained it. Now, being streetwise and on the ball and knowing he would 'go down' for receiving stolen goods, my friend told them he had found it in his cab and was going to drop it into his local police station on his way home. So they asked him which one, for a future check, and let him go.

Needless to say, his local nick was expecting him as he walked through the doors in the middle of the night and the sly looks between the two sides as the forms were filled out said it all. The Old Bill knew he was at 'the trick' and that they couldn't touch him. And my mate knew that they knew he was going to get the 'hooky gear' back in three months' time, because no 'owner' could possibly claim something that had not been stolen!

Now here's the punchline, and it's as sweet as a nut. After about a month or so, my mate assured me, he got a letter from the Lost Property Office saying his lovely mohair suiting had been claimed by a passenger in his cab! This is the beauty of the sting somebody perpetrated on him. If my mate had protested and said it wasn't found in his cab, he would have been charged with receiving stolen goods. So, as they say in the cab trade, he had to 'wipe his mouth' and walk away!

The coppers at the desks at most police stations hate to see a cabbie come in with lost property, especially late at night when they are trying to get their heads down. They have to sort every item into plastic bags, then fill in the large forms in triplicate and they get the right moans. I've even had some of them tell me to hand it in at my local nick, or dump it if it's only an umbrella! So when we had trouble with the Law in our local cab shelter many years ago, we decided to get our own back. A young copper had been nosing round the shelter late at night, then coming in with cab numbers and informing the drivers, who were all eating their grub, that their cabs were on an official taxi rank and the first two should be available for hire. This irritation went on for a few nights and, even though the young copper was right in his literal interpretation of the law, it was 3 o'clock in the morning and not a living soul in sight! So, for the next three or four nights, very late at night, a queue of serious-faced cabbies could be seen in the local nick, handing in dirty old socks and soiled towels as lost property. The desk sergeant, who normally was having a nice kip at this time of night, went ballistic – the queue of cabbies was never-ending. A couple of nights later a police inspector came into the shelter with a big grin on his face and said, 'Okay lads, we'll call it a draw. The young constable is now at another nick!' The new bobby on our beat was well-behaved and often came into the shelter for a cup of tea and a fag!

But, things are changing swiftly at the PCO now that they are under the control of the Mayor and 'Transport For London'. Hopefully, they will be able to sit down with all the trade organisations and work closer with them and to get rid of some of these very annoying anomalies. The PCO need to recognise that the London cabbies want to work with them as partners.

VICTORIAN CABBIES

The following excerpt from a Government White Paper of 1895, entitled 'The Cab And Omnibus Trades', makes for interesting reading:

The cabman's trade is one to which all sorts of men find their way. Many an educated man, who can do nothing else to earn a living, can drive, and if put to it will seek his daily bread in this way. In the strike of 1891, it was by a man of University education that the books were kept. Cabmen have plenty of opportunity for reading the daily papers for discussions amongst themselves, and as a result are generally up to date in general information, and often keen politicians, many being members of Radical clubs. It is these men, one hears, who are the most conservative of all on trade questions. Many again, are prominent in their temperance or religious views, and one cabman is well known as a secularist lecturer on Sunday in the parks.

By constant contact with all kinds of people cabmen become very observant, and often know more about those they drive than the latter imagine. Moreover, a certain confidence is reposed in their discretion and many a doubtful piece of business is transacted under their eyes – not indeed that there would be such evidence as would even warrant them in making their suspicions known, but about which they have little doubt in their own minds. The relations between the cabmen and the public they drive are, on the whole, very pleasant and if at times they become otherwise the fault is not always confined to the side of the cabmen.

Health

The principal diseases from which cabmen suffer, namely rheumatism, bronchitis and chest complaints generally, are those due to exposure to the weather. These diseases are aggravated by indulgence in strong drink, a habit which, as already indicated, is prevalent, although there are, on the other hand, not a few abstainers and a flourishing temperance society among their numbers. It must, however be said that the publicity to which the men are exposed, and the fear of having their licenses endorsed, prevent a good deal of excess. A cabman may drink, but he must on no account get drunk. The mortality returns, so far as they can be applied to this trade, do not give it a favourable position for longevity. . . .

Cut out the bit about the booze and hardly anything has changed for over a hundred years, has it?

The total demise of the horse-drawn cab took place over a period of ten short years, basically 1904–14, with the once famous Hansoms declining at a rate of 1,000 a year. Thousands of them were sold for firewood at £1 each. The internal combustion engine had arrived on the scene, not without a few hiccups. In 1897, fourteen electric Bersey cabs left the depot of the London Electric Cab Company in Lambeth. They weighed 14 cwt and could propel the cab, with two passengers, for 50 miles without having to recharge their forty accumulator cells carried in a tray beneath the body.

These electric vehicles didn't last too long and were replaced by fifty others, supposedly of a better design. But they kept breaking down and cabmen were reluctant to drive them. In 1903, the first petrol-engined cab, the Prunel, was licensed to ply for hire in London. They soon disappeared, but the breach in the dam had been made and more models began to make their appearance: Vauxhalls, Fords, Rationals, Heralds, Argylls and Unics were all on the road by 1906. By early 1907, they had been joined by a variety of others: Renault, Adler, Mascot, Adams, Hewitt, Simplex Sorex and Jeantard.

It's strange to think that, in 1907, five hundred Renault taxis, the largest fleet of motor vehicles anywhere at that time, left the premises of the General Cab Company in Brixton Road to ply for hire on the streets of the capital, thus pushing the cab trade forward. The company's chairman, Mr Davidson Dalziel MP, later to become Lord Dalziel, was severely criticised for going 'foreign'; not only were the vehicles French, but most of the company's capital came from France. It's desperately sad for me writing about the late Lord Dalziel, because our lovely eldest daughter Jenny lies in peace in the shadow of his mausoleum in Highgate Cemetery.

Yet some fifty years later, another fleet of Renaults was launched by Welbeck Motors as the first minicabs on the streets of London, thus threatening the very existence of the cab trade and pushing it backwards!

How London came to produce the finest taxi service in the world, with the most professional and highly trained drivers, is a complete mystery, according to Philip Warren in his book. The trade has been shot at from all angles since before the First World War and successive governments, both Tory and Labour, have cynically denied cabmen their proper fare increases enabling them to earn a decent living. *The Times*, in an editorial of January 1912, said, 'The cabs in London are the buses of the Parliamentarians who had control of the fares they paid.'

London Buses were the ones who always seemed to get the goodies, and have done since they started. Zero-rated VAT, subsidised diesel and many other perks. Yet these are now private companies paying out annual dividends to their shareholders. What on earth can be the thinking behind zero-rated VAT for buses – and for passenger jets – yet no zero-rated VAT for taxis? I think Philip Warren hit the nail on the head when he described the reasons being the very powerful 'Omnibus Lobby' and the 'friendly' MPs, who were paid 'consultancy' fees in the past to ask questions in The House on behalf of their lobby!

UNITED IN THE PAST

Certainly, the cabbies in the past fought long and hard for their living against these people with vested financial interests in putting the Omnibus Service before cabs. Nor were they afraid to take on their guv'nors, the LMCPA, the London Motor Cab Proprietors Association – or even the Government, if they thought they'd been hard done-by. A disagreement arose in 1912 over who should keep the 'extras' on the meter, that is the charges for extra passengers, luggage, etc. that, historically, always went to the cabbie. But the LMCPA were desperate to keep their companies solvent after the refusal of the Home Secretary, Winston Churchill in 1911, to grant an application for a fare increase. The proprietors, in their wisdom, had decided that the extras, amounting to £50,000 per annum, should rightfully belong to them. Within a few weeks of that decision, some 15,000 drivers, mechanics and washers were on strike and the LMCPA garages were at a complete standstill. The cabbies eventually won the battle after a long and bitter fight.

The following year, the cabbies went on strike again. This was known as 'The Petrol Strike', because petrol had risen from 8d to 1s 1d per gallon. The LMCPA announced that the drivers would have to pay the full amount of the increase, a rise of 1s 3d a day on their petrol costs, representing a 20 per cent cut in wages. After nine weeks of the strike, some companies began to capitulate and came to private arrangements with their drivers for the original price of 8*d* per gallon for their petrol. A few days later, on 23 March, an agreement was signed by all the parties for a return to work. The cost of the three-month strike had been enormous. The Union had paid out £40,000 in strike pay and the owners had lost over £1 million. But the London cabbies had shown that they had spirit and wouldn't be trodden on, either by their bosses or the Government.

THE DUNLOP TAXI-DRIVER OF THE YEAR COMPETITION AND TRADE FAIR

Way back in the late sixties, one of the best-known cabbies in the trade was Joe Polski. Joe spent most of his spare time collecting for various charities and was deeply involved with the British Legion. In fact, he had the honour of carrying the banner at the annual Remembrance Day march-past at the Cenotaph. So when, sadly, he died, other leading charity collectors wanted to keep his name alive in the trade. After many meetings and careful consideration, they decided to organise an annual event in his memory and call it the Taxi-Driver Of The Year Competition, in aid of the Joe Polski Memorial Fund.

The first competition in 1972 had humble beginnings. The venue was Jubilee Gardens, next to the County Hall and now the site for the London Eye. In effect, it was little more than a village fête with all the wives setting up stalls and selling *bric-à-brac* and souvenirs, all for charity. In those early days the charity had no major sponsors, in fact hardly any sponsors at all, except maybe the radio circuits and trade organisations. But, and all credit to them, from day one up to the present day, the PCO examiners always gave up their Sundays to organise the driving tests. The format hasn't changed much over nearly thirty years. You sit the written test about two weeks before the final competition, all multiple-choice questions on London and the cab trade, and the best thirty or forty go through to the big day.

The first section on finals day is the obstacle course. Hundreds of gaily coloured bollards are laid out to create tight hairpins, narrow garages to reverse into, plus a difficult slalom course to negotiate. Points are deducted for every bollard you hit. The final section used to consist of being handed an envelope and inside were a dozen different destinations. After being checked out of the arena by a marshal adjusting your meter to a stop-clock (no waiting time registered), it was up to the contestants to try and sort out these destinations into the shortest possible route. Marshals checked you in at every point and the contestant with the lowest amount on his meter, won the section. The total points over the three sections were added up, with a prize to each section winner, and the best overall score became Taxi-Driver of the Year. I always entered the competition every year, not that I was any good at it, but because I wanted to get the feeling of the day for my regular piece in the trade press.

The competition started getting bigger every year and finally moved to the Guildhall Courtyard in the City.

Something very strange happened in 1978. I made the final again and, instead of knocking down the bollards like skittles, as per my usual style, I had a clear round and went into the 'mystery tour' leading the field. Again, many of my fellow contestants helped my cause by getting lost on the final section. In fact, two of them never returned to the arena! So, much to my surprise and utter delight, I had won the competition by a mile. Not that the prizes in those days were much to write home about. I think I got a new set of tyres and a few bits and bobs, but I was champion for a whole year. I remember we turned up late for the presentation buffet and, would you believe, I got lost and all that was left for us to eat was a plate of crisps!

My very first duty as Taxi-Driver of the Year was to drive in the Lord Mayor's Show, following the Lord Mayor's coach as a back-up in case of a breakdown. For more than twenty years I've had to live with that old saying, 'After The Lord Mayor's Show . . .'. My wife and three kids were very excited that I was in the show and asked if they could sit in the back of my cab. So I thought to myself, why not, they can only say no. Much to our delight the organisers agreed. That was the very first and last time the winner of the Taxi-Driver of the Year Competition was allowed his family in the taxi for the Lord Mayor's Show. And didn't my kids enjoy it? They still talk about it to this day!

Being Taxi-Driver of the Year proved to be very profitable for me and very high-profile for the charity. I got myself invited on to the TV show *Blankety-Blank*, way back when Terry Wogan was compère, and won the star prize. I made a documentary about cabbies for the BBC and another for Tokyo Television. I did a Saturday night show for ITV where the contestants stood up and announced themselves: 'My name is Joe Bloggs and I'm a window cleaner.' The panel of celebrities all had to ask questions and find out the real 'Joe Bloggs'. Even then my luck held out and I won the star prize, because the comedienne, Maureen Lipman, one of the panel, lived close to me and after I told her the number of her flat, next to where we lived, she convinced the rest of the panel that I must be the window-cleaner!

The day after the ITV show went out, I received a phone call and this American voice was on the line saying how he'd watched the show and enjoyed my cockney humour. 'Would I,' inquired the voice, 'come on to an American chat show with Burt Reynolds?' Now I knew this had to be a wind-up by some of my friends, so I was trying hard to recognise the voice and saying, 'Is that you Terry, or Bill, or Harry?' Finally the penny dropped and I realised it was actually the producer talking to me! All I had to do was to meet the film crew on a boat by Westminster Pier and tell a couple of funny cab stories to Burt Reynolds. They were all falling about in fits of laughter and amazed that I could tell funny stories without the aid of cue-cards. I left within the hour and the boss shook me warmly by the hand and gave me a very large US banknote for my performance. I had a great time in my year 'on the throne' and I like to think I helped to make the competition better known to more people.

In the early eighties the competition really took off when it received major sponsorship from Dunlop and, after many different venues, it finally found its true home at Battersea Park. You've got to hand it to Dunlop, they've sponsored it ever since. Nowadays, the prize money of around £4,000 and even the prizes for section winners are well worth challenging for. Then, in the nineties, the Committee decided to include a Trade Show in the day's event and suddenly the cab manufacturers were there and the meter people, the insurance companies, the radio circuits and just about every ancillary back-up to the trade. The original 'village fête' had progressed into a major event and looked set to get even bigger every year.

As for the guys in the cab charities who first mooted the idea, well, they're getting a bit long in the tooth but they're still working extremely hard every year without any financial reward to make the competition even bigger and better. I must just mention two of the major players on the organising team who were there at the very beginning: Bill Tysack and his wife Gracie have worked their socks off for their charity over the past thirty-plus years and the London Taxi-Drivers' Fund for Underprivileged Children has benefited from their considerable input. Their dedication was finally rewarded by Her Majesty The Queen with a British Empire Medal for Bill. Well done to Bill and his wife Gracie, and long may you be involved!

Sunday, 1 September 1997, and I was making my way once more to Battersea Park to cover yet another Dunlop Taxi-Driver of the Year Competition for my paper. As soon as I arrived, I knew that something had happened. The place was almost deserted and all the people I spoke to were looking glum and dejected. Finally, my wife phoned me and said she was too upset to come to the show. Only then did I discover that Princess Diana, her boyfriend Dodi Fayed and their chauffeur, Henri Paul, had all been killed in a tragic night-time accident in Paris. The show limped on, but it really was a lost cause and eventually spluttered to its close, with only a handful of the expected visitors arriving.

This is an extract from my editorial following the tragic death of Princess Diana, and it indicates the deep sadness felt not only by Londoners or the British people, but by the normal, average person, male or female, from all over the world. With the added benefit of hindsight, the media have decided that this public outburst of sympathy was nothing more than a whipped-up frenzy and unreal. I think not, I was there!

HALT Magazine Editorial, September 1997

Many millions of words have been written about the tragic death of Diana Princess of Wales and written much more eloquently than I could ever hope to write.

But this editorial is intended to be something different. It is a humble dedication to the loss of a lovely lady, written by a hard-nosed London cabbie who has roamed the streets of our great city for many years. Like most mature cabbies I thought I had heard it all and seen it all. The terrible news of President Kennedy and Martin Luther King's assassinations, the state funerals of the King and Winston Churchill, and standing outside Buckingham Palace as a wide-eyed kid, watching the VE and VJ celebrations to end WW2.

Believe me, those momentous events pale into insignificance compared to the days leading up to the funeral of Princess Diana. I and many other London cabbies were madly busy taking distraught people – with their flowers and their Teddy Bears – to Kensington, Buckingham and St James's Palaces all through the day until the roads were closed. London was an absolute madhouse. Wealthy travellers were coming into Heathrow from all over the world and hiring taxis to take them to one of the palaces with their flowers. Then getting the taxis to take them back to the airport, before flying home again. There were endless queues of people – all carrying their floral tributes, patiently waiting for taxis at every single main-line railway termini. These people certainly weren't exhibitionists hoping to get on the telly. They were ordinary folk – just like you and me, coming from all over the UK to pay their last respects to *their* Princess. The outpouring of grief was truly unbelievable. Not only were the ladies weeping in the back of the cab, so were hard-nosed businessmen. Even after the funeral, the crowds were still flocking to London, especially to Kensington Palace, the former home of Princess Diana. It was reported that the floral tributes were five feet deep and that 10,000 tons of flowers would have to be moved eventually and would probably take a team of volunteers up to one month to clear!

But the memory that will live forever in my mind, was the sad, sad day of the funeral. The route of the cortège on its journey to Northamptonshire was scheduled to head north up the Finchley Road, just a couple of hundred yards from my home. I stayed with my wife to watch the funeral on TV and when the cortège left Westminster Abbey after a very moving service, we all decided to walk down to the route and pay our last respects. That walk down Heath Drive was truly amazing. One minute it was all deathly quiet and peaceful, then suddenly, almost as if somebody had rung every doorbell in every house in the street, the doors opened and masses of people joined in the sad march to the funeral route. It must have been the same story in every single side-street leading to the route of the cortège. Everyone wanted to pay their last respects to *their* Princess!

THREE

THE BUTTERBOY

Every new London cabbie is known by his/her fellow drivers as a 'Butterboy'. My friend Philip informs me this nickname comes from the old Victorian cabbies who only came into London during the busy summer months and were nicknamed, somewhat sarcastically by the regular cabmen, as 'Butterflies'. In effect, they flew in, nicked all the work and flew out again! Through the ages, this term became 'Butterboys'. That's something else I've learned. I always thought it was a derivation of 'Butt-a-boy', while others told me it's derived out of jealousy by the older drivers, such as 'taking the bread and *butter* out of my children's mouths'. Whatever the explanation, I was a Butterboy and fiercely proud of the fact. My record had been closely scrutinised and I was considered 'a fit and proper person to drive a licensed taxi', albeit always 'at the discretion of the Commissioner'.

The very first taxi I drove was an Austin FX3, the cab with a open luggage compartment on the left of the driver. The FX3 was a good cab to drive and quite nippy, with good steering. The problem was, it was so perishing cold in the winter you needed long johns to keep you warm. One of the tricks of the cabmen to help keep him warm was to pull out the heater pipe that warmed the passenger area, then plug it into the driver's section. So the cabman got all the heat. Even then, it was still bloody freezing! And as for stopping, that was another problem. The old-fashioned rod brakes weren't too efficient and tended to pull to the right or the left when braking sharply. My particular cab had a quaint tendency to swerve to the left, so I used to put the 'anchors' on, then turn the steering wheel to the right to compensate. The taximeter was something else in those days. Would you believe you had to wind it up at the start of your shift? Another novelty on the FX3 was the four jacks that could be pumped up by an outside handle. Many's the time I came out of a cab shelter late at night, started the cab, put it into gear and realised some of the lads had jacked it up. It's a weird experience putting your foot down on the accelerator and not moving an inch, while all the lads were standing outside the cab shelter, roaring their heads off. I remember stopping once in my FX3 when this lady flagged me in Kentish Town and then proceeded to jump into the luggage compartment! I got a fit of the giggles and told her she was allowed to sit in the back!

I had roamed the streets of London for nearly a year painstakingly learning the Knowledge in theory. Now I had made it as a fully-fledged London cabbie,

I needed to learn it in practice if I wanted to earn a decent living. First and foremost, I needed to learn how to get in and out of the main-line stations and where the taxi ranks were situated. Next, it was knowing when the boat trains arrived at Liverpool Street or Waterloo, because they were the best trains of the day, full of wealthy Americans who might require to travel anywhere by taxi in Greater London. I well remember in my early days of cabbing, when I reached the 'point' (the head) of the taxi rank at Waterloo Station. The drivers behind me suddenly started blowing their horns for me to cross over to the smaller rank outside the station exit. I didn't know about the smaller rank and what they were all hooting about, so I just panicked and pulled out.

Then again, Paddington Station was a real bind if you ranked up not knowing when the Cornish Express or another of the expresses was due. In the old days, once you were ranked up in Paddington, you couldn't pull off. Talking about Paddington Station still brings a shiver down my spine because of my lucky escape as a Butterboy. It was a Sunday afternoon and I was about third cab on the rank. A couple of guys came up to the first driver – we were all standing around talking – and asked for Epping Forest. He turned it down, as did the second cabbie as, apart from not liking the look of them, he thought they looked a bit dishevelled. It was also too far for me, because I intended finishing in an hour. So I also turned it down. The guy behind me didn't want to go, but the next cab said he'd be pleased to do it because it took him home. Sadly for him, these two guys were desperate escaped prisoners and they shot him to death in Epping Forest. I was absolutely horrified when the news broke about the callous murder. But, like most other human beings would, I thanked God it wasn't me.

Another thing you needed to learn in those days was to tip the 'waver uppers' at Victoria and Kings Cross Stations. These were old boys trying to get a crust. They would stand on the corners of St Pancras Road and Wilton Road at Victoria, with a rolled-up newspaper in their hand, and wave up the next cab around the blind corner when a space was available on the station rank. All the drivers used to give them a few coppers for their trouble. If you were doing night work, it was imperative to find out the times of the 'theatre burst'. Most of the theatres turned out within an hour of one another. So you would work one theatre until it was dead, then dash round for the next one to burst. That was always the busiest time for London cabbies; taxis were often very scarce at the burst and drivers tended to turn out their 'For Hire' signs and sort out the best-looking fares. The wealthy, streetwise Americans soon cottoned on to this practice and often you would see a Yank and his lady, standing about in Shaftesbury Avenue, with the guy holding a five pound note up in the air. They soon got a taxi!

I recall early in my cabbing career picking up a fare in the West End late one Saturday night. I only worked one night, and he wanted to go to some little village in Kent. He looked okay, so we did a deal and he paid half up front with cash and a cheque for the other half after we had completed the hiring. With the benefit of hindsight, taking a cheque probably saved me from going to prison! Let me explain. We eventually arrived in this sleepy little village in the early hours of the morning. He paid me off and I kept the engine running, because it was winter and I didn't want to trust my luck with the battery, while I got out of the cab and relieved myself against the rear wheels, which is allowed by law!

It was a pleasant journey back with a pocketful of cash and no traffic, and as I was poodling down the Old Kent Road I heard the sound of police sirens behind me. So I slowed down and pulled towards the kerb to let them go by. But the two police cars didn't go past me. One pulled in front, blocking me in and the other pulled up tight behind so I couldn't reverse away. Well, the next couple of hours was really like a cops and robbers film and it's only now I can laugh at it. Mind you, at the time, I almost needed bicycle-clips at the bottom of my trousers! Two huge coppers jumped out of the police car in front. They dragged me out of the cab and held me face down over the bonnet. Then a plain-clothes officer, smelling like a brewery, bent over me and snarled, "Ave yew by any chance just come from a village in Kent called ——?' 'Yes,' I stuttered in reply, 'I dropped a fare there and I'm just on my way home.'

The plain-clothes officer stood up in triumph and, just like the blustering detective in the hit TV police comedy, *The Thin Blue Line*, said to one of the coppers in uniform, 'I fink we've got our man, Smith. Git into the back of the cab and tell this piece of shit to drive to the Borough nick.' By this time I was absolutely terrified. No, I thought to myself, it can't be *Candid Camera*, can it? But what have I done, why are they arresting me? So I drove down to the Borough nick and into the courtyard. The large copper in the back got out, then pulled me out. 'Keys to the boot,' snarled the detective, holding out his hand in an aggressive manner. He went to the back of the cab, opened up the boot and pulled out my golf clubs. 'Ah ha,' he said smiling in triumph as though he'd discovered the Crown Jewels, 'and what have we got 'ere?' 'I think you'll find they're called golf clubs, officer,' I replied politely. Seeing the other coppers chuckling and him losing face, he suddenly grabbed hold of me and sticking his beer-smelling breath close to my face, snarled, 'Oh, I see, we've got a piece of shit 'ere who finks he's a bleedin' comedian, is that it?'

Suddenly I wasn't scared any more. I hadn't done anything to break the law, yet this ignorant pillock was treating me like a common criminal. 'Look officer,' I said, 'I haven't done anything wrong, yet I've been arrested and dragged out of my cab in the middle of the night. Why don't you just tell me what the problem is without acting like James Cagney all the time?'

Well, I thought the guy was going to burst a blood vessel and he stepped menacingly in front of me. Luckily, out came another plain-clothes man who was obviously a senior detective and he beckoned me into the police station and led me into a little interview room. 'I'll tell you what's happened, son,' he said, sitting on the chair opposite me and lighting up a fag. 'There has been an armed robbery in this little Kent village and somebody's clocked your number as being at the scene of the crime.' So that was it. I explained about the fare and about relieving myself against the cab and I showed him the cheque for half of the fare. He took the cheque from me and obviously went to phone my passenger to confirm my story, because I had insisted my fare put his name and address on the back of the cheque. He came back into the room a few minutes later with a big smile on his face. 'Okay, son,' he said, 'it's all been a big bloody cock-up and you're free to go. Pick up your golf clubs and your cab and go home and have a good kip, you must be knackered.'

So that was that. No apologies for the way they had manhandled me and no apologies for the abuse that had been handed out. I had the last laugh though. Old 'smelly beer-breath' was still standing by my cab with the big, burly coppers. 'I'm on my way home now, officer,' I said in my smuggest voice. 'But you're in trouble with your guv'nor, you're in for a right rollicking.' The two burly coppers laughed, a little too heartily, but I left a bit sharpish before 'old beer-breath' blew a gasket!

NIGHT WORK ON THE CAB

My kids were little, my wife was overworked, so it seemed the best bet was to work at night and help her out in the day. That was the theory, anyway! As it eventually turned out, I went training over Hampstead Heath twice a week and played golf twice a week. My neighbours must have thought I was a burglar or something, because I never left home in my car until around 8 or 9 o'clock at night. Come 2 o'clock in the morning, I could always be found in one of the famous old cab shelters, drinking tea and eating something really unhealthy. Forty years ago, the work on the streets at night enabled taxi-drivers to get a decent living in six or seven hours of non-stop driving. Then, unfortunately, another two hours or more were spent chatting in one of the cab shelters. But the cameraderie among the night drivers was truly amazing. Everyone knew everyone else and, if any of the guys were in trouble, either with ill health or financial problems, they would have a whip-round and everyone chipped in what they could afford. A lot of that cameraderie has unfortunately all but disappeared in the frenetic pace of today's world. The young cabmen are up to their ears in debt, paying big mortgages and hefty repayments on new cabs, and they are chasing the dough from the start to the finish of their shift. And at the end of a long shift they are tired out and just want to go home to bed, not sit around nattering.

Coupled with the cameraderie was learning the unwritten rules of the cab trade. You never picked up a fare within 50 yards or so of a 'loaded' cab rank. You never overtook an empty cab and picked up a fare in front of him, and you always let a hired cab pull out from a side street if you were empty. In fact, you would always let a cab out, because nobody else would! In the old days, if you ignored these unwritten laws, you were very likely to be pelted with copper coins by the other drivers and called some choice names. Sadly today, some of the youngsters may well overtake you, going like a bat out of hell, and nearly take your bonnet off when they swoop in front to pick up a fare. The saddest thing of all, though, is that they don't understand what you are talking about when you remonstrate with them. In fact, in today's aggressive society, you may well get a mouthful or cop a right-hander for your troubles!

But all in all I thoroughly enjoyed doing night work on the cab for twenty-odd years and, as a well-known trade journalist, the tales I was told gave me some great copy. One of the best storytellers in taxi-driver's shelters was known as 'Tom the Fib'. Tom got his nickname because he tended to make up little white lies that made his stories even funnier. He had a quickfire delivery, told almost totally in Cockney rhyming slang, coupled with racing slang. When the punchline finally arrived and most of the shelter went into convulsive laughter, it used to take me some little time to translate the rhyming slang!

This is one of his stories told in Tom the Fib's parlance, with the translations to help!

My trouble's (trouble and strife – wife) been giving me plenty of aggro lately. I promised to pick her up in the sherbet (sherbet dab – cab) and run her to Uncle Bob's (the pawnbroker's) to buy some tom (tomfoolery – jewellery). You know what these Richards (Richard the Third – bird) are like. She's panicking, 'cos she's holding a monkey (five hundred pounds) in her sky (sky-rocket – pocket) and she's 'eard from the neighbours that some drummers (burglars who knock on the door), are working our manor (area) and they've marked 'er card (picked her out as a likely victim).

'As it 'appens,' he went on, to his captive audience, 'I 'appens to trap (pick up) a flyer (an airport job) . . .

so I'm running well late and after dropping off the punter, I looks at my kettle (kettle and hob – the old fob watch) and decides to give her a ring on the dog and bone (phone). But all she does is laugh when I apologise for being late. She tells me that a firm of drummers have turned over (robbed) my drum (house) while she'd been out shopping. What a liberty, they've even gone up the apples (apples and pears – stairs) and 'alf-inched (pinched) my brand new whistle (whistle and flute – suit), my camel-haired smother (overcoat), and even my lovely crocodile St Louis (St Louis Blues – shoes), my strides (trousers), and my pure silk almonds (almond rocks – socks).

Now Tom is reaching his punchline and he's got the audience giggling loudly, he knows he's got them in his hand. He stops, with what I believe is called a pregnant pause, then continues: 'I don't mind too much them nicking that gear, 'cos it's all on tick (hire purchase), so I ain't gonna pay for it anyway. But what d'ya reckon those thieving little toe-rags done next? They went into the bog (toilet) and nicked my spare set of 'ampsteads.'

Well, the guys were falling all over the floor unable to control their laughter. As for me, I'd completely lost the punchline because I couldn't translate 'ampsteads. So, I asked the bloke next to me, what in Heaven's name were 'ampsteads? ''Ampsteads, are Hampstead Heaths,' he replied with a look on his face that said 'Where are you from?' 'Hampstead Heaths are teeth, you know, false teeth that you leave in the glass, got it?' he said, in a somewhat tetchy manner.

The old cab shelters were wonderful places to relax after belting around the streets of London all night and some of the characters you met in them were unbelievable. Many of them had their same seats, every night of the week, for years and years. I'd go to sit down somewhere and the blokes would shout out, 'Don't sit there, mate, that's Bill's seat (or Len's seat) and they won't like that.' 'That's tough,' I would sometimes say, 'there ain't any more seats, so they'll have to lump it.'

These regulars would come in as I was eating my dinner and give me a perishing look. Then they would stand drinking their cups of tea, mumbling to each other, until I had finished. One night in the sixties we were all sitting in the Pont Street shelter, just off Sloane Street. The door opened and in came a handsome, Arabic-looking man wearing a startling white dinner-jacket. I thought his face looked slightly familiar as he spoke. 'Would one of you gentleman please take me up to Les Ambassadors Club?' he said in beautiful English, with a very slight accent.

All the boys were busy eating and larking about telling jokes and one shouted out, 'We're 'aving our dinner, guv, so you'll have to try and get a passing cab.' Suddenly, the penny finally dropped and I put a name to the face: Prince Aly Khan, married to the gorgeous filmstar Rita Hayworth and the son of the Aga Khan, the very rich and powerful owner of all of those racehorses. Oh so very casually, Prince Aly Khan pulled out his wallet and, flourishing a five pound note in the air, said, 'Gentlemen, whoever finishes his dinner first can take this as a reward.'

I tell you what, I nearly got trampled in the rush to get out of the shelter. That fiver represented the best part of a night's work in those days and the shelter emptied like magic in seconds. I never did find out who did that job!

The Pont Street shelter was also the place where we first formed a Cab Golf Society. Tony Jacklin had just won the British and the American Open Golf Championships and suddenly taxi-drivers were into a real 'gentleman's' game. We called our society the Cadogan because it sounded very posh and certainly nothing whatever to do with common cabbies. Would you believe, because of the class barriers in those days, we made a rule that none of our members should go to a tournament in their cabs. If they really had no other form of transport, we would all meet outside the golf club and pile into one or two cars for the final lap. I recall once we were having dinner at the snooty St George's Hill Golf Club, near Weybridge in Surrey and one of the old colonial 'colonels' was remonstrating in a rather loud voice with a pretty young waitress, going on and on about the way his dinner had been laid out. 'My dear gel,' he was heard to say in a patronising manner, 'what on earth am I supposed to do if my potatoes have been put on top of my meat?'

We were all sitting there feeling embarrassed for the young girl, who hadn't laid out the old duffer's dinner in the first place. Suddenly, one of the wags in our Society shouted out: 'Why don't you lift the potatoes, guv, and take a one-shot penalty, without moving them nearer to your greens?'

Even the snooty members laughed loudly and the old 'colonel' didn't say a word! We never went back again.

In the seventies there was a well-known conman who used to prey on cab drivers and many of the older drivers will well remember his patter. In fact, it's an even-money bet that many of them were actually conned by him! He was good, in fact he was very good. How do I know? Suffice to say I had him in the back of my cab one evening, and if it hadn't been for the fact that I had just started work and only had a bit of cash in my float, I would probably have been conned as well!

The conversation would start with him dropping the names of all the villains at the time. He knew Jack Spot and Albert Dimes and Ronnie and Reggie Kray, and he often shot over to Spain to have a chat with Ronnie Knight and the rest of the boys. Then would come the sting – and all the guys tell it the same way. 'Would you be interested in earning a quick wunner (a hundred pounds)?' he would say. Well, who wouldn't like to earn a quick wunner, thought all the guys, so they were hooked. Then he would direct them to a side-street and point out a particular car. 'See that motor there?' he would whisper in a secretive manner. 'That's got twenty grand in the boot, but it's broken down and I need some readies to hire another motor.' He was quite cute, he never ever said if the money was stolen. But if somebody asked to check the boot for clarification, he would suddenly look over his shoulder and say, 'You can if you want to, pal, but if the Ol' Bill are clocking it, you could go down for a stretch.'

Before he was finally arrested, I did a piece about him in the trade press and the letters I received from hard-nosed and streetwise cabbies, all pleading for anonymity, of course, had to be read to be believed. Most of them had coughed up £40 for the hire car, a lot of dough some thirty years ago, while one had actually parted with his wedding ring and every single coin in his money bag! This particular guy had dropped him at Hertz Rent-A-Car near Victoria Station very late at night and watched him go through the door with his £40. After a long dwell, the cabbie went inside to find him only to discover from the guy behind the desk, that he'd left by the back door! Another writer said that he was about to give him the £40, when someone walked past and opened the car door that supposedly held the twenty grand!

I went to court when the conman's case came up and after pleading guilty to dozens of offences against cab drivers, the judge asked him why taxi-drivers. His reply was an eye-opener: he said, 'Taxi-drivers are so flash, they think they know everything. But when they get conned they won't tell anyone 'cos it means a loss of face and that's more important than the money.' He then promised to resume operations when he came out of prison.

Then there was the lady who used to phone the Warwick Avenue Rank at around 9 o'clock every evening. I happened to be on the back of the rank one night drinking a cup of tea and still a Butterboy. I should have guessed something when the guys in front of me came up all giggling and asked if I would like to pick up Miss X from Elgin Avenue. They all pretended they were playing cards and just like the proverbial Butterboy, I fell for it. Miss X was a big, buxom, good-looking woman. A bit past her sell-by date for sure, but well made-up and wearing a very expensive, full-length fur coat and glamorous high-heels. Probably an ex-showgirl, I thought to myself.

'Once round Regents Park please, driver,' she said in quite a refined voice, 'and then we'll come back again.' Funny destination, I thought. But it's none of my business where she is going, 'cos she's paying the fare. So we were halfway round the Inner Circle in Regents Park and she shouted out, 'Could you please stop a minute, cabbie?' So I pulled up the cab, leaving the engine running. Suddenly the lights went on in the back of the cab and she shouted out again, 'What do you think of this, cabbie?'

I turned around in all innocence and was confronted by this lady who had pulled open her full-length fur coat with not a stitch of clothing on underneath. I remember thinking at the time in my embarrassment, 'I bet you don't get too many of them to the pound.' I mumbled something in reply like, 'Very nice, Madam.' It was certainly only for looking and definitely 'ne touchez pas'! Then, it was lights off in the back and the return to Elgin Avenue with not another word being said.

I often think about that lady – not her nudity of course, but how lonely she must have been getting her kicks by exposing herself to London cabbies. After all, she was a good-looking woman, very smartly dressed and obviously had a few quid. As a Butterboy at the time I thought it was all a right giggle. But as I matured, I often felt sorry for her and wondered what might have become of her.

All the boys were still drinking tea outside the Warwick Avenue shelter when I returned and you can just imagine the ribald remarks shouted at me. It was almost like an initiation test at an Officer's College or the like. I had passed the test with flying colours because I had enough bottle to come back to the rank and suffer the remarks thrown at me. I suppose you could say that was my formal acceptance as a fully-fledged nightman.

Many of the guys I used to play football with in the taxi team called Mocatra (Motor Cab Trade) used the long-gone Leicester Square cab shelter. As I recall, most of them were Jewish and they had a method of working a cab that fascinated me. They would graft really hard through the summer and all through the Christmas holidays and New Year's Eve. Come the first week of the new year, off they would go to the Canary Islands until Easter, completely missing the dreaded 'Kipper Season'. Again, I don't believe anyone knows the origins of this expression, it has just evolved through the mist of time. It could well mean as flat as a kipper, because, in the old days, January through until March was as dead as a doornail for us cabbies. Our season really started to get off the ground with the Ideal Home Exhibition in late March, followed by the Chelsea Flower Show. In-between times it meant mooching around the streets of London, desperately searching for a fare. And God help any of the gents in St James's who had the temerity to take out his handkerchief to blow his nose. I've seen these people immediately surrounded by three or four empty cabs!

One of the most notorious cabbies in my early days was known to each and every nightman as 'Claude the Bastard', and he was well named. When the cabs started ranking outside theatres waiting for the burst, just as the doors opened Claude the Bastard would come zooming down the outside and blatantly nick a fare. He would then proceed to do exactly the same at every other theatre. How he didn't get a smack off a cabbie, I'll never know. Another one of his tricks was to hang up by the bus-stops outside Green Park Station in Piccadilly in the evening rush hour. He would work his way through the long queues asking people if they wanted to share a cab to Victoria at two bob a person. When he finally had a cab full – and I mean full and well over the legal limit – off he'd trundle to Victoria. Then it was back again for another sort out on the rank. I reckon he could load up about three times in the rush hour and at around fourteen bob a journey, that was good money, even though he could have got nicked for touting. The Bastard is probably long dead by now and even though he was despised by his fellow drivers and very aptly named, I still thought he was quite a character in his own way.

But back to the story about the Canaries and the boys missing the Kipper Season. Back in the sixties, the Canaries and other such exotic locations hadn't even been discovered by the tour operators. So the lads went down to the dock next to London Bridge and took a banana boat to Tenerife. They reckoned they could live comfortably in Tenerife on five bob a day (25p). Another major bonus was all the rich widows living out there enjoying the winter sunshine, probably on their old man's insurance money. The tales they told when they returned at Easter all bronzed and healthy had to be heard to be believed. Some of them enjoyed 'tea and sympathy' and free board with the same wealthy widows every winter! I believe they described themselves as 'directors of a transport company'!

THE GIRLS ON THE GAME

The law banning prostitution from the streets had been passed a year or so before I got my badge. But it was still commonplace to see all the 'girls' standing in Bayswater Road, Sussex Gardens and, of course, all around Wardour Street, Brewer Street and Old Compton Street in Soho. People told me that ordinary housewives from Wales and up North used to come down to London on the game for the weekend on the pretence of having a part-time job. As a Butterboy, I still didn't know the ropes about this seedy nightlife. I must have been very naive in those days because it took me weeks to realise that the instructions from a 'lady' with a gent to go 'once around Hyde Park' meant anything of any significance. The penny finally dropped with the vibrations in the back of the cab! I really should have tumbled to what was going on earlier, because the 'ladies' always called me 'darling' and made the gent give me a ten bob note. This was all about learning to be streetwise the hard way and, if the police had been on the trail of this 'lady', I, in my innocence, would have been well and truly nicked for procuring,* or the like.

From day one, I was basically an honest and hard-working London cabbie, proud of what I had achieved and still remembering the cold fear of being charged and thrown into the same cell with the notorious Kray twins. But – and I don't knock it – there were many cabmen who worked with the girls and the seedy Soho clubs to bring in the punters. They earned a lot of money, but many lost their cab licences more than once. These late-night cabbie characters were very, very shrewd. They even learned foreign languages to converse with the punters – especially French – and their favourite plot was bang opposite Raymond's Revue Bar in Brewer Street. They would approach a likely-looking group of guys and ask them if they were after a good time. The problem for the new faces on the block trying to get in on the act, was that some of these likely-looking groups were the Ol' Bill in plain clothes, and they were promptly nicked for touting and lost their licences for periods of up to a year or more. Mind you, even forty years ago, these guys would expect a couple of quid for taking a punter to one of the girls and probably 7s 6d a head (37½p), from one of the many clubs that offered cabmen a regular commission for each new guest. 'Italian' Dom and his mates worked the clubs all night, then finished up taking the hostesses and their gentlemen friends back to their apartments in the small hours of the morning. When a famous nightclub came under new management back in the sixties, the new boss decided in his wisdom that they were famous enough not to need the help of cabmen bringing in punters. So he cut out paying commission on new guests, without realising the power of the taxi grapevine. I believe they went skint within the same year, even though he took an expensive ad in one of the national papers, threatening prosecution against cabbies for telling his prospective punters that his club was closed for re-decoration! When in Rome. . . .

If you reckon a nightman could net about twenty-odd quid a week in those days, then finding a boozy group who wanted a bird and a club was very remunerative for a night's work! Some of my favourite stories of working nights revolved around a well-known lady of the night, known to us as 'Miss Bunny'. Many of the more mature cabmen reading this section will remember her well, especially as she used to pay the cabbies a massive three quid per punter at the time. That meant a four-hander could net you half a week's wages in one hit.

Miss Bunny's flat was in Mayfair, about a pitching-wedge distance from Saville Row police station. She and her maid had their system down to a fine art. You rang the outside bell and said who you were, then climbed to the top of the stairs. Another door and another bell. Then the maid answered the door and blokes tell me that she was so ugly, I think the phrase they used at the time was 'She looked like an advert for keep death off the roads'. Many a punter would recoil in horror at seeing her boat-race (face) and want to leave, thinking this was his surprise for the next half an hour. But the guys used to reassure them she was only the maid. Then they were ushered into the front room to meet Miss Bunny, a very buxom French lady, who came out in her sexy lingerie, gave the nervous punter a friendly kiss to make him feel at ease, then whisked him into her boudoir. The cabbies were given a cup of tea and, because she was the only lady in London who did business on a Sunday night, they settled down in comfort to watch *Sunday Night at the London Palladium* on the big colour television. I am reliably informed by my friends, because, of course, I was never there, that sometimes there used to be as many as six punters and six cabbies all sitting watching the TV at the same time. That's democracy for you! Next came the superb organising skills of Miss Bunny that made certain of no aggro, or monies, going astray. After her 'services' had been completed, you could hear her start washing her hands in the bedroom sink. This in turn made the Ascot heater in the kitchen begin to let off steam, and that was obviously the pre-arranged signal she had got her money safely and the maid could now pay off the cabbie. The maid expected a tip of half-a-crown per punter (12½p), so everyone was happy, or so I am informed!

I think one of the best stories I ever heard about Miss Bunny was when a cabbie arrived at her door with *five* strapping Canadian oil-riggers. She didn't bat an eyelid and proceeded to call them in one at a time for a 'service', then completed the job in less than an hour! The guys were more than satisfied with her services and wanted to go on to a nightclub. So the cabbie had copped his commission from Miss Bunny and doubled it by taking them to a club. What a great night's work for that lucky cabbie! Around the mid-seventies, I heard on the grapevine that Miss Bunny was selling up and buying a château in France. She was greatly missed by all us nightmen, because she was a real grafter and very fair. I'm sure many of her punters will miss her as well for the sheer dedication she showed to her profession. I often wonder if the local French villagers know the real profession of the 'lady in the big house'?

Come the end of the seventies, the girls on the game had all but disappeared off the streets and were paying the 'carders' to plaster their services in phone boxes. Some of the girls could still be found in various pockets around London, like Goodsway at Kings Cross, made famous in the film *Mona Lisa*, starring Bob Hoskins and Michael Caine. Then, for a time, Endymion Road opposite the old Harringay Stadium became a haunt for the girls. And you'd still find a few trying their luck around Sussex Gardens in Paddington. But most of these are young kids with a habit and the old grafters are long gone. Escort agencies seem to be the modern way around the old law, and while many of them are exactly what they call themselves, some of the more shady ones provide much more than an escort!

But with the benefit of hindsight it's very naive for governments to think that any sort of legislation can completely eradicate what is probably the oldest profession in the world. There will always be a need for prostitutes, whether on show or underground, and some of the more liberal countries like Holland have recognised that need and legalised the profession for the health benefits of the clients. If some men need to pay for these services, then they deserve to go with a clean, healthy woman. I certainly wouldn't advocate going that far in the UK. But we need to get away from the old Victorian thinking: keep it a secret and if you don't know about it, then it's not happening!

My one endearing memory of night-driving in the sixties and the seventies is heading down York Way towards Kings Cross in the early morning for a late cup of tea, and seeing dozens of taxis parked in the kerb with their 'For Hire' signs flashing on and off like Christmas lights. These guys worked for Levy's, a big cab garage at Kings Cross, and in those days everyone was 'on the clock', that is, they got a percentage of the clock – plus their tips. But, after midnight, when most of the coppers had gone for their cuppa, many cabbies tended to 'stalk' the fares for an hour or so. 'Stalking' – again, I don't know where the expression came from – meant doing the fares after switching off the meter, thus copping the whole amount. The drivers normally told the punter that the meter had gone up the creek and this was his last fare before he went back to the garage.

So, when it was time to finish, they would all park up, hit the meter a number of times to give the guv'nor some 'one and ninepences'. That way he wasn't too suspicious about the low meter returns, compared to the high mileage. I don't think anyone is on the clock today. Most drivers now rent 'on the flat'. That means paying a weekly flat rate and using the cab as a family car as well. This system is very popular with the guys, because once the cab starts playing up, you just take it back to the garage and change it. The one downside to this system is having to pay your weekly rent whether you are working or not.

Unfortunately, with rising inflation over more than three decades, the prices of cabs – and the flat rate to hire them – have gone up alarmingly. When I think that my first cab on the flat was eleven quid a week, it's almost like a joke. The youngsters of today are paying upwards of £170 a week for a decent cab, and a lot more if they want a nearly-new one. But that's inflation for you. My first brand-new taxi cost me the princely sum of £1,200; now, nearly four decades later, a new cab costs around £30,000. So it becomes a vicious circle. The young fella has got to get his cab money first, then his mortgage, then the clothes and food for his kids, so the pressure is on from the time he leaves home. And if it's quiet on the streets, then he's struggling and under stress.

I well remember when the flat rate system was first suggested and the union turned it down. In those days, most of the cab garages in the East End, the traditional home of cabbing, were strictly T&G (Transport and General Workers Union; Cab Section) and, unlike today, you couldn't hire a cab from them unless you were a union member. By today's laws, they would be conceived as illegal closed shops. But they were the union's power base and had been for many years, and trying to introduce a system where the driver probably only showed up once a month, or for a service every few months, might prejudice their membership. And so it proved. The flat rate became so popular that practically every cab garage got on the bandwagon. And why not? They were guaranteed a set amount every week and the regular practice of stalking went out of the window overnight.

But the wise old heads in the union had called it right in the beginning. Next to the minicab menace, the flat rate was possibly the very first poison arrow shot into the trade's vital organs to create disunity. No longer did the cabbies come into the garage every evening and every morning to pay in their money. No longer did you give the washer, or the guy who checked your oil, 'a drink', then have a cup of tea and a chat with your fellow drivers. It became every man for himself and screw the union and any other trade organisation trying to get members. So, the new boys coming into the trade – especially the large influx in the seventies – soon learned their apathy from the more mature drivers. It was a cavalier attitude adopted by the newly-qualified cabbies. They had completed the Knowledge and now, presumably, the world owed them a living. Why bother to join a trade organisation or a union, or a licensed radio circuit? Why bother about minicabs, or touts, or any Government legislation detrimental to our trade? Just go out on your cab, keep your nose clean and take your money. Whatever happens, people will still need London taxis! That's true. But would you believe it was possible to take more money on the cab over twenty years ago? It will be interesting to see if history agrees with my premise!

FOUR

ECCENTRICS AND FAMOUS FACES

Back in the early sixties there seemed to be a proliferation of eccentrics all over London and many of them favoured London taxis as their mode of transport. But in today's modern world, with everyone flying about at a hundred miles an hour, apart from the odd pop star strutting his stuff in the tabloids and talking about his/her conquests, all the rest appear as clones. Most of the old eccentrics were Colonel Blimp-like characters, still wrapped in their comfortable timewarp of colonial rule and the heady days of the Raj.

One of the best-known eccentrics of the sixties was a popular broadcaster and peer of the realm, known to everyone as 'Bob'. This gravel-voiced Lord was the very first on any TV producer's list when it came to discussing politics in any shape or form. And to give him his due, he was very lucid and informed. But the word around the cab trade focused on his liking for a bevvy, he did like a drink! Anyway, one lunchtime many years ago, I was cruising up St James's Street waiting for their Lordships to leave their clubs and the doorman on the Carlton Club flagged me down. 'You've drawn the short straw,' he said with a smile on his face. 'It's Bob and he's had a skinful.'

I shrugged my shoulders as if I wasn't too bothered and said to the doorman with a laugh, 'What's new, pal, at least he can hold his booze and never lungs up in the back of the cab.' Then out strolls Lord Bob, puffing on a big cigar and wearing the big spotted bow tie that was his trademark. 'Evening News, please, cabbie,' he slurred in his famous gravel voice. Well, that's what I thought he said anyway, as I made my way towards Fleet Street. Suddenly there was a loud bang on the partition window and the sound of this loud gravel voice yelling out in anger, 'Where are you going you blithering idiot? I asked for Ebury Mews – in Belgravia!'

There wasn't a lot I could say, so I just touched my forelock in a subservient manner and mumbled, 'Sorry, m'lud.'

I was a great advocate of two-way radio and promptly joined a radio circuit at the very start of my cabbing days. I firmly believed that by having every London taxi on the radio, we could combat the ever-growing threat from unlicensed minicabs. Our biggest account was the BBC at their new TV Centre in Shepherds Bush, so famous faces in the back of my cab were two a penny. I and my colleagues carried all the stars every night of the week and, generally speaking, the bigger the star the nicer the person. Lovely people like Max Bygraves, Tommy Cooper and, most of all, Les Dawson, who would turn the air blue in the back of the cab with his 'Lord-Mayoring', as would Johnny Speight, the creator of the lovable bigot Alf Garnett. Johnny, the talented son of an East End Docker, lived out by Greenford and you always had to stop at a Chinese takeaway on the way home. I liked Johnny, he was one of us. You could often see his white Roller at night parked outside the White Elephant, the old gaming club that used to be on the river in Grosvenor Road. His personal number plate always gave him away. MOO 1: remember what Alf Garnett used to call his wife – 'Silly Moo'.

But, strangely enough, many of the top comedians of the day were really miserable people. Frankie Howerd, who lived in Pembroke Square just off Kensington High Street, was a strange character. If you tried to have a friendly chat with him, he'd say rather rudely, 'Please don't ask me to tell a funny gag, for God's sake.' Benny Hill, who lived around the corner from Frankie, was very quiet and shy and never said a word during the journey. Even the ebullient Kenneth Williams, who lived next to the White House in Osnaburgh Street, never ever spoke in his funny voice and he always looked so terribly distressed and thin and unwell. Since their death, it turns out that they all had a sexuality problem. But the Goons really were nutty eccentrics. I remember picking up Spike Milligan, Harry Secombe, Peter Sellers and Michael Bentine one summer's day and taking them to Palace

Court in Bayswater. They had the rear windows of the cab fully down and for the whole journey, all I could hear was loud Goon-type noises directed at the pretty girls.

It always makes me giggle when I think of the time I was driving slowly into the TV Centre and this little souped-up Mini shot past me like a bat out of hell. As I pulled alongside him by the main entrance, I shouted out sarcastically, 'Who'd'ya fink you are, bleedin' Stirling Moss?' I gulped in embarrassment when the familiar bald head appeared and the scarred face gave me a wicked look, with just the faintest of a twinkle in those cold, blue eyes. Yes, you've guessed it, it really was Stirling Moss!

Lester Piggott, the famous – and very wealthy – jockey, who finished up doing a stretch in prison for tax evasion, had the dubious reputation among London cabmen of being the meanest passenger of all time. I picked him up once in Mayfair and took him to one of the posh restaurants. I was chatting to him and trying to get some good tips for the gee-gees and he was reasonably friendly. I think the fare was about four and sixpence (23p) and he waited for his sixpence change out of the five bob. 'Is that my "drink", Lester old mate?' I said, deliberately holding back the sixpence. His eyes turned very steely, he obviously didn't think much of my joke, and he said in his funny grunt, with no roof to his mouth, 'Yew got the fare uh, I not a charity.'

Strangely enough, it was soon after that incident that these cards suddenly started being given out

1. Our lovely daughter Jenny, to whom this book is dedicated. Sadly, she died of breast cancer on 27 December 1999, at the age of forty-one. Jenny is shown here meeting Michael Aspel after I had won the Taxi Driver of the Year competition.

2. My family are now committed to supporting breast cancer charities. My son Nick and daughter Jo are shown in the centre. Nick's wife Rose is on the left; Jenny's husband Keith is on the right. They raised about £1,200 when they did this run.

3. Girl power on the Knowledge. Lady drivers make up only a tiny percentage of London cabbies. Just 50 or so among a total of some 22,000!

4. Two young women studying for the Knowledge outside the Knowledge Point School, Caledonian Road, London. Until the Sex Discrimination Act came along the London cabbie was a male institution – a bit like the Long Room at Lord's.

5. The lads are learning as well. The Knowledge is taking longer – anything up to four years. Both guys and gals need part-time jobs just to exist.

6. My son Nick, in younger (and hairier) days, passes the Knowledge some thirty years after his dad. Now turned forty and with a wife and two kids he sports a severe crop.

7. Studying for the Knowledge is hard work, requiring concentration and cooperation, and also supplies of tea and biscuits.

8. A Hansom cab, or as Disraeli called it, 'The Gondola of London'. With a top speed of 17mph a Hansom cab still couldn't go flat out in today's traffic.

9. London's first cab shelter. Sadly, because of all the road and traffic changes in London, a mere thirteen remain out of forty-seven.

10. The Bersey electric taxi. The massive batteries made this an extremely heavy 'old boy'.

11. One of the very first motorised cabs: the start of a variety of different makes – and the knacker's yard for the poor old horses.

12. The proud author receives his award for winning the Taxi Driver of the Year competition. Even now, twenty-four years on, I still believe someone bribed the other contestants to take a dive. . . .

13. Me and my cab, sponsored for the Underprivileged Children's Charity. The charity's committee work like dogs all the year round, and with no stand-down money.

14. Driving in the Lord Mayor's Show as Taxi Driver of the Year, with my wife and three kids in the back. This was the first and only time that a winner was allowed to put his family in the cab.

15. A transatlantic taxi tête-a-tête – one of New York's Yellow Cabs meets one of London's Cabs for charity. It was a great fun day and I enjoyed it – but I'd sooner drive a *London* cab!

16. David Wilkie, Olympic Gold swimming champion, taking part in a charity event with me and other taxi-drivers. Today I'm quite a bit heavier round the midriff but I've still got all my hair – sorry David!

17. The prize of fame: chatting to Michael Aspel before appearing on his show as Taxi Driver of the Year. I enjoyed all the chat-shows. Give me a mike and I'll talk all day!

18. The FX3 was my first cab. Several (with their proud owners) are pictured here outside London Taxis International taking part in a display to celebrate the building of the first FX3 back in 1948. To the far right are pictured Barry Widdowson, Managing Director of LTI (left) and Andrew Overton representing Mann and Overton.

19. The old Beardmore taxi, now defunct. I ordered their new four-door model from the Clifton Hill garage in St John's Wood in the mid-sixties. But they closed down soon afterwards.

20. Roger Rabbit, alias London cabbie Del McCarrick.

❊❊ The Royal Bank ❊❊ of Scotland	◉ LEUKAEMIA RESEARCH FUND
	2nd July 1998
PAY Leukaemia Research Fund	
Eight Thousand Pounds	£8,000
Del McCarrick	

21. Roger Rabbit unmasked, with Frank Bruno. Del has single-handedly raised almost £100,000 for leukaemia and breast cancer research.

22. The Russell Square cab shelter, one of the liveliest shelters in the daytime. Many of the clientele honestly believe their discussions benefit from the close proximity of the university!

23. The Russell Square shelter has been in place since 1901, thanks to Sir Squire Bancroft, and has been preserved by the efforts of the Heritage of London Trust.

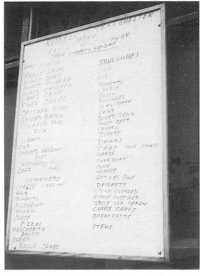

24. The Russell Square cab shelter menu – featuring those well-known gourmet delights, oemellets and tomattos.

25. 'One shilling per mile' – one of the selling points to get people to switch to the new minicab service, as shown on their 1961 business card. Most of us cabmen knew they couldn't make money with that tariff – but it was a sprat to catch a mackerel.

26. The Renault Dauphine, introduced as a minicab in 1961, shown without the Air France livery that would be introduced later.

27. Cabbies picket County Hall over minicabs in the 1970s.

28. You wait ages for a taxi and 300 come along at the same time – the fares demo in Whitehall in 1978.

29. The LTDA fight the good fight.

30. Steve Norris, then Minister of Transport for London, meets members of HALT Ltd.

31. Heathrow was only a temporary tent village in 1946, but there were comfortable chairs, a bar, cable facilities and a W.H. Smith & Son.

32. Next to Heathrow's temporary tents, there were red telephone boxes and a mobile post office.

33. Moving on from tents, if a new Terminal 5 is built at Heathrow, it could look like this.

34. The Queen and the Duke of Edinburgh inside a new 'green' Metrocab gas taxi.

35. Actress Joanna Lumley launches the first TX1 model taxi in 1997.

to cabmen by many punters, basically saying that they didn't believe in tipping because they thought everyone was entitled to a living wage without begging.

The bigger the star, the nicer the person. But at the other end of the scale, you also had to suffer the new kids on the block who thought that one hit record made them top of the pile. One such person, a female singer, was always on the cabbies' blacklist. She used to come out of the BBC's hospitality room most nights, drunk as a sack, and proceed to shout out at the waiting radio cabs in a shrill voice, 'Which one of you bastards are going to take me to Blackheath without "effing" charging me double the "effing" meter?' I often wonder how she ever got home, but she occasionally makes a comeback.

The BBC Television Centre at Wood Lane in the sixties was a world unto itself. I honestly believe the staff were programmed into believing that the Director General, or the DG, as he was called in reverent whispers, could well have been on the same plane as one of the Royals. This reverence manifested itself one evening while I was sitting in the reception waiting for a fare. A very smart, elegant, elderly gentleman approached the desk and asked to speak to the Director General. Well, the lady behind the desk nearly had a touch of the vapours. People couldn't just speak to the almighty willy-nilly, said the look on her face. 'And who shall I say is calling, sir?' she asked, with a sour look on her face. 'Could you tell him it's King Gustav of Sweden,' said the elegant gentleman. The lady started working her buttons and obviously got through to the DG's private secretary. Putting her hand across the phone to cut out the sound, she enquired in a loud, rude voice, 'I'm sorry, sir, who are you the King of?'

Another eccentric was dear old Lionel Bart, the song-writer. He could be seen in all his glory nearly every day of the week, driving his open-topped Bentley around the West End, smoking a large cigar and wearing a huge, white stetson-type hat. Lionel was a likeable, talented but gullible guy from London's East End. When he went bankrupt, even after the rip-roaring success of the musical *Oliver!*, both on stage and in film, the Jewish guys in the cab trade felt an affinity to a fellow East Ender. In cab parlance they all agreed that the money-men had really done him up like a kipper. If I were to include all the weird characters I had met as a cabbie over the past forty years into a comedy script, the producers would send it back as unbelievable and not real life. Take the dear old clergyman who hired me outside the Athaeneum Club in Pall Mall one lunch time. 'Find me a shop, my man,' he said, 'where I can get some cough medicine for one of my horses, and I'll reward you with a bottle of my best claret for your troubles.' You just can't make up situation comedy like that. It either happens in real life, or it doesn't! On another occasion, I picked up these two dear old American ladies at Paddington. They were from the Deep South and their accents were a combination of mint juleps and *Cat on a Hot Tin Roof*. 'We wanna go to Buck-ingham Pal-ace, honey,' said one of the ladies in a deep Southern drawl. 'I tell you what, honey,' she went on, 'there's a nice big tip in it for yuh, if yuh can show us yuh Queen.' I just grinned to myself and mumbled something about trying my best as I headed down Park Lane. How can you explain that even as a thirty-year-old Londoner, I'd never seen the Queen in person? I started chatting away to them, and as we passed the lights at the bottom of Constitution Hill – bang outside the Palace Gates – a large policeman stepped into the road holding his arm up to stop me. My immediate reaction was, have I been caught in a speed trap? But no, I noticed the Royal Car was on its way out. As it slowed down alongside my cab, I said in a very laid-back and nonchalant voice to my passengers, 'Get your cameras out, ladies, and give a nice big wave to the Queen and the Duke of Edinburgh.'

There was a long, southern squeal from the back and it felt like the cab might turn turtle as they dashed to the right-hand side and started leaning out of the window taking photos. Both Her Majesty, wearing a lovely ball gown and a tiara, and the Duke gave them a friendly wave, which caused more large squeals. I followed the Royal Car and the police outriders as it went down Birdcage Walk towards Parliament Square. I recall the Royals were attending some sort of function that evening at the Royal Festival Hall on the South Bank. Once again I was stopped by a copper at the junction of Horse Guards Avenue, this time to allow the Queen Mother and the Prince of Wales to go past. They were obviously heading for the same venue and had come from Clarence House. 'The big maroon car coming out on the left in front of us is carrying the Queen Mum and the next King of England,' I said casually.

Again, there was mayhem in the back as the two old ladies stuck their heads out of the nearside window, even exposing their Southern bloomers in their excitement! They were shouting out and clicking their cameras, totally overawed with sheer joy. I got a big kick out of it as well. Even I had finally seen the Royals for the first time in my life!

Even when we returned to Paddington Station, they were still buzzing with excitement. They paid me off handsomely, then asked for my name and address. 'When we-all get home, honey,' said one of the ladies, 'we gonna tell all our friends that we know a London taxi-driver who can show them the Royal Family, if you give him a big tip.'

I appreciated the money, but I didn't have the heart to tell them the truth and spoil their Royal dreams!

Some of the older drivers will confirm another long-gone oddity that used to occur at Christmas time around the gentlemen's clubs in St James's. The cabbies were often given bottles of wine and, in my own experience, braces of grouse or pheasants from their country estates, that looked awful and smelt even worse! When you're a 'peasant', you don't appreciate the taste of game birds and I stopped taking them home after my wife dumped them. Even our old cat wouldn't eat them!

While on the subject of Christmas, I recall sitting

on the old taxi rank in the middle of the road in Kensington High Street one Christmas Eve in the mid-sixties. The phone rang and when I answered it, a very posh voice said, 'Could you please come around to Kensington Palace as promptly as you can?' And I, in my ignorance, replied, 'Wot d'ya mean, guv? The KPH?' That was the cabbies' nickname for the Kensington Palace Hotel. 'What on earth are you talking about, man?' said the posh voice, slightly irritated. 'I mean *the* Palace to pick up Lord Snowdon's father.' At last, I thought to myself, I'm going to come face to face with some real royals. So I turned left into the private road that leads to Kensington Palace, made famous the world over with the tragic funeral of Princess Diana some three decades later. The copper on the gate waved me in and I did a U-turn and stopped outside the front door. One of the flunkeys, all done up in his very distinctive livery, came out and told me they wouldn't be long. Then out came Lord Snowdon. I recognised him because as a professional photographer he used taxis quite regularly. He was talking to an old bloke who didn't look too good, that was obviously his dad. The next person to appear was none other than Princess Margaret, with a couple of toddlers. The thing I noticed about her at the time, and something I've never forgotten, was her make-up. I would think it was proper theatre make-up and she'd possibly just come back from a big 'do' where she'd been wearing a high-necked ball gown, or the like. But it could have been yesterday it's so clear in my mind. This brown make-up finished in a line halfway down her neck and the rest of her neck was lily white!

Anyway, they all got into the back of the cab and started kissing and cuddling the old boy. Then, when they got out, he directed me to the London Clinic. I read in the papers a few weeks later that unfortunately the nice old boy had died. As for me, it was a wonderful Christmas story to tell my kids. Not too many dads have had a real live Princess in the back of their taxi!

But, it was mainly at night that the eccentrics really used to come out and some of the tales told in cab shelters seemed hard to believe. It appears that this certain Lord had a fetish for being beaten up and there were two cabmen I knew well, who took it in turns to accommodate him. They used to call him Mister Whippy and, it seems, they were well paid for their services. One of the guys, I believe his nickname was Violent Pete, used to hold court in the shelter after his sessions with Mister Whippy, while we listened in awe. 'So, I knocks on the door of his big gaff in Holland Park,' says Pete, 'and as soon as Mister Whippy opens the door, I hit him straight in the moosh. There was claret all over the shop when he hit the deck.' 'So what did he do when he got up?' asked one of the chaps, his eyes popping out. Pete laughed at his admiring audience and, taking a puff on his cigarette, he replied in a nonchalant voice, 'You ain't gonna believe this, guys. The geezer gets off the deck, sticks a fiver in my hand and, as he's wiping the claret off his boat, says, "That was wonderful, Peter, I do hope you can make it again tomorrow night." '

Well, that brought the house down and the guys were falling about trying to comprehend such a weirdo. I believe Violent Pete carried on providing this service for his gentleman until the sad day when Mr Whippy was found dead in his house, murdered by one of his weird contacts, who maybe went over the top.

Violent Pete and his mates were a randy bunch. They would work until the early hours of the morning and then 'plot up' outside the Leicester Square cab shelter, now long gone since the square was pedestrianised. They often picked up foreign au pairs, or young ladies of the night who didn't have the price of a taxi fare home, and both parties would come to a working arrangement on how the fare should be paid. One of Violent Pete's randy mates came into the shelter one night and said he was a bit concerned about the rash coming up on his tackle. So, we told him to go to the all-night VD clinic that used to be in the old St Paul's Hospital in Endell Street, Covent Garden. He was shown into the clinic and seen by a young Chinese doctor, who made him drop his strides while he examined the rash closely. Looking up with a deadly serious expression on his face, the young Chinese doctor said quietly, 'You taxi-driver, yes?' The driver nodded, fearful that the doctor had spotted a fatal and rare VD strain only found in London taxi-drivers. 'So,' said the Chinese doctor, 'how much you charge me from here to Golders Green?'

Well, Violent Pete was holding court in our shelter one night and telling the story of how he chatted up a gorgeous Malaysian girl who wanted to go to Maida Vale. Now, to really appreciate the following story, you need to know that Violent Pete was a racist, a xenophobe and a homophobe. He hated blacks, any kind of foreigners and detested what he called 'filthy iron-hoofs', or 'poufs'. I remember Violent Pete's radical anti-gay stance way back in the sixties. The taxi shelter where we all gathered every night used to have an open toilet next to it, one of those old-fashioned walk-in ones with no roof. At night, this became a major meeting point for many an aristocrat who had learned his fetish at his public school, and some of the young Guardsmen from the barracks up the road, attempting to improve their meagre army pay. Late one night, Violent Pete pulled up and went into the loo before having his dinner. Well, to cut a long story short, he of all people saw a strange-looking person in the shadows of the loo, and, believing it to be one of the regular aristocrat gays doing a bit of cottaging, Pete rushed into the shelter like a man possessed, shouting, 'There's an "effing" pouf next door and I'm going to do something about it.'

This brought a ripple of laughter from the rest of the guys in the shelter. Most of us, myself included, had an attitude of live and let live. But Pete was notorious for his homophobia and when one of the wags shouted out, 'How much did he offer you, Pete?', this brought the house down and sent Pete over the top with rage. He dashed to the corner where the shelterkeeper kept a heavy steel bucket for the tea-leaves, or the 'grouts' as we called them. This was way before the invention of tea-bags! He grabbed the heavy steel bucket, dashed next door to the urinal and the next thing we heard was a dull thud, a scream of pain and the sound of a steel object hitting the ground. Pete, in his vile rage and with the loss of face among his mates, had lobbed the heavy bucket, half full with tea-leaves, over the toilet wall and clonked the 'gay' full on the head. A minute later, the shelter door burst open and in came a guy with his lovely coat covered in tea-leaves, as far up as his astrakhan collar. Much to our amusement, he waved his warrant card at us, proving he was the Ol' Bill, and yelled out like a raving lunatic, 'What dirty bastard did this? The nick sent me here to clear out the poufs and this is the thanks I get.'

Anyway, back to Violent Pete's sexy story about the gorgeous Malaysian girl. 'So,' said Pete, 'I gets to her gaff and she's telling me she's a model and would I like to come in and have a butcher's (butcher's hook – look) at her model photos.' All the boys are sitting around listening intently and hoping Pete comes out with a saucy sexy story.

'Anyway,' says Pete, 'one thing leads to another and we start having a kiss and a cuddle.' He paused for a moment, took a drag on his ciggie and continued.

'We're both getting a bit excited,' said Pete, 'so I started stroking her undercarriage to take the situation one step farther. But, I was absolutely gutted when I felt somefink that a woman shouldn't have and I yelled out in anger, you're a bloody geezer and I'm groping an "effing" pouf.'

This brought the house down because Violent Pete had been well and truly taken in by a 'Lady-boy'. Nobody dared call him his new nickname to his face, but from the day of that incident, everyone referred to him as Violent Pete the Lady-boy.

As the years evolved, I got to know Violent Pete pretty well and, to be perfectly honest, I quite liked him. But he certainly was a catalogue of contradictions and a positive menace to himself. On the plus side, he worked tirelessly for the trade charities, collecting monies and organising dinners and dances. And, when it came to organising, he was the top man. Loan Clubs, Sick Clubs and Football Syndicates were his forte.

But on the minus side were his vicious and uncontrollable rages – hence his nickname. He was a big powerful man, very fit and a good all-round sportsman. He liked the ladies and the ladies liked him. But heaven help the person who happened to upset him for some, often trivial, reason. His face would suddenly contort into a frightening sneer and his brilliant blue eyes would stare balefully at the perpetrator and you could almost see the red mist totally consume him. I recall one night in the cab shelter, way back, we were discussing football and a young Butterboy had the temerity to insinuate that our syndicate wasn't quite kosher. In effect, an accusation that the organiser – guess who – was at the hey diddle-diddle.

What happened next was like a bad American gangster movie. Violent Pete grabbed hold of this young fella, hit him with a crushing right-hander that immediately broke his jaw. And if a crowd of us hadn't dragged him off, he would have certainly throttled the guy. Yet within a couple of minutes of the mayhem, the red mist had lifted, just as quickly as it had descended, and Violent Pete came out of almost a trance, filled with a feeling of deep remorse.

Another time he came into the shelter late one night, showing his bruised and bloodied knuckles. It appeared that a couple of drunken yobs had attempted to get into his cab while he was at the traffic lights. Naturally, Violent Pete had told them in no uncertain terms where to get off! Anyway, as he pulled away, they aimed a couple of kicks at his cab and shouted abuse. Now, most people, myself included, would have wiped their mouth, as we say in the trade, and driven off. But not Violent Pete. He did a left into the next street, got out the starting handle and waited for them to appear. He then jumped out of the side-street like an absolute nutcase and proceeded to beat the shit out of them, breaking numerous bones in his frenzy. Now don't get me wrong, I'm not being flippant and trying to trivialise violence, in fact I believe violent people are possessed with a terrible curse and are to be pitied. All I am doing is attempting to describe the true events in my own prose.

After a week had passed he assumed, quite wrongly as it happened, that he was in the clear. Then, not long after that, a knock on his door and it was the Ol' Bill come to arrest him. And they threw the book at him. Actual Bodily Harm, Grievous Bodily Harm and Assault With a Deadly Weapon. It appeared that a married couple were having it off in the back of their car nearby and they had seen everything. The delay in reporting the attack stemmed from the fact that they weren't married to each other and, obviously, they didn't want to get involved.

I was reliably informed at the time that the Ol' Bill had him bang to rights as they say and Violent Pete looked like going down for a long stretch. Who helped Violent Pete to beat the rap? The two guys, covered in bandages and plasters, stood up to give evidence and, instead of just relating the events, thus ensuring their attacker would go down, they started shouting out abuse at Violent Pete and threatening to do him in after the trial. The judge had no alternative but to throw the case out, because now it seemed like a case of self defence.

I haven't seen Violent Pete for many years. But if he happens to read this book, I reckon I will get a visit very soon!

Back in the sixties, most of my cabbie mates worked for W.H. Cook and Sons, a large cab garage, long since gone, in Ivor Place behind Marylebone Station. We all played soccer for the taxi team and gathered in the café outside the garage every Wednesday. It seemed that every Wednesday, when we were larking about in the café, these two cracking girls used to walk past. One had a blonde bubble cut and was very shapely, while the other was a sexy-looking brunette. It goes without saying that the café used to empty while the guys shouted various remarks at the girls in their oh-so-tiny miniskirts. One of the regulars told me they lived around the corner in Huntsworth Mews and were high-class call-girls. Quite a number of times we'd see the two girls go past in a big car driven by a handsome-looking guy with sunglasses. Imagine our surprise when the Profumo Affair made the headlines, nearly bringing down the Government. John Profumo MP was Secretary of State for War at the time and had told a fib in the House of Commons, denying any involvement in the goings-on at Cliveden. But, and this is what ruined him, it was alleged a Russian spy was also enjoying the fun and games with the same lady at the same venue. And there, splashed across the front page of every newspaper, were the two girls and the handsome guy with the sunglasses. Namely, Christine Keeler, Mandy Rice-Davies and Stephen Ward! I thought after the hubbub had died down that Stephen Ward was made the fall guy in the whole affair. Just being faced with a ridiculous charge of living on immoral earnings was enough to ruin his smart practice in Harley Street. But for him to take his own life before the trial was even over didn't ring quite true to me. Who knows, maybe he just knew too much about too many important people. The press, maybe on orders, blew the affair up to be just a sex scandal among the rich and famous. But later evidence that has come to light sounds a more serious note about espionage and Britain's security. The rumours were rife at the time about the strange goings-on at Cliveden and dozens of household names were being bandied about as to their possible participation in the fun and games. But only one name constantly came up as to the identity of the man in the black mask. But that was nearly forty years ago and today those sort of fun and games are considered the norm, or even slightly old-fashioned! It's nice to know that John Profumo's wife, the former film star Valerie Hobson, stayed by him through those terrible times. It's also gratifying to hear that both of them have been doing good work for the underprivileged people of the East End.

Returning to the subject of the cabbie's football team Mocatra and my involvement in the team for many years, way back in the early seventies, we arranged to play a charity match at Hendon Stadium against the ShowBiz XI. Most of their team were as good as gold – especially their Captain and goalkeeper, Ed 'Stewpot' Stewart, the Radio 1 DJ. But not Kenneth Cope, who at the time had a starring role in the popular detective TV series, *Randall and Hopkirk (Deceased)*. He had supposedly been killed in the series, but rejoined his partner from the spirit world as a ghost. Anyway, Kenneth Cope became a bit self-important after the match and, poking his head around our dressing-room door, shouted out, 'Is there a back door out of this place, so I can dodge all the waiting autograph hunters?'

Now, there's one golden rule when you are in the

company of quick-witted cabbies. Never feed them a line like that! As quick as a flash, one of the wags replied, 'You shouldn't have any problem, pal, just walk through the "effing" wall!'

A short memo to Colin Welland, co-star of TV's first popular soap, *Z-Cars*, and now a successful scriptwriter. Do you recall me taking you from the TV Centre to Granada's HQ in Golden Square in the seventies? Well, guv, you were two bob short of the legal fare and if you're reading this book, thirty years' interest on two bob works out at about fifty quid, okay!

MR X

I've mentioned many eccentrics, or weirdos, as they may well be termed today. But 'Mr X' was something special and warrants a special sub-chapter in my recollections.

The story goes that he was the heir to a vast fortune, but, because he was the black sheep of the family, they had given him an A1 account at Coutts Bank (unlimited funds) and shipped him off to London. He appeared late one night at the doors of a posh little hotel in Belsize Park, asking for a room. By all accounts he looked a bit unsavoury and the receptionist called for a porter to eject him. Now comes a classic example of revenge being sweet. Mr X traced the owners of the hotel the next day and promptly bought the place, lock, stock and barrel. He returned the following evening with the former owner and sacked every member of the staff, whether they were involved in rejecting him or not. He then took on new staff, reserved the top flat for himself, and registered as an account customer on my radio circuit.

It wasn't too long before Mr X became the most talked-about taxi punter in the whole of London. His antics and strange behaviour even raised the interests of the Sunday tabloids, following an article I wrote about him in the cab trade press. He had this habit of jumping out of a cab, like a bat out of hell, and shouting to the driver, 'Wait for me!' And because we all know he had unlimited funds and paid twenty-five bob an hour waiting time (£1.25 in modern money, but a fair rate some thirty-odd years ago), all the drivers waited. Now came the problem. The drivers waited and they waited, and they still waited. Often the hours turned into a full day, and in one extreme case, the waiting turned into a whole weekend. That extreme case is a classic and needs to be told just to be believed.

Mr X hired his account cab one Friday evening and asked to be taken to Charing Cross station. Because he was as nutty as a fruitcake, he had this annoying habit of sitting near the open partition behind the driver, constantly looking at his watch and shouting out at regular intervals things like 'Change down to third gear and keep to twenty miles an hour up to the next lights'. And on, and on and on. The regular drivers just used to bite their tongues and take no notice of his weird antics. So the cabbie pulled into the forecourt at Charing Cross station and, crash, the doors burst open and out jumped Mr X at breakneck speed, like a man possessed. 'Wait for me!' he yelled, disappearing into the station.

So the driver waited all night and in the early morning phoned his dayman to relieve him. The dayman waited all Saturday, then he phoned his nightman for relief. Anyway, this went on until Monday morning, when Mr X arrived back at Charing Cross, would you believe, in another taxi. He had been to Brighton for the weekend and his train had been diverted on his return into London Bridge station. He then proceeded to get a taxi to Charing Cross, where his cab had been waiting for him since Friday evening! I believe someone told me the waiting time was in the region of £85, a lot of dough in those days.

It was odds-on that, because I lived in this area, I would be picking him up quite often. That's exactly what happened one winter's night on my way home at around 2 a.m. I came in for the job and the little old boy who used to do the night despatching said to me in his fruity Cockney accent, 'Listen 'ere, me old mate. You know this geezer is as nutty as a fruitcake and you know you might be with him till tomorrow night?' 'Yeah, that's all right, John,' I replied, 'I've had a bad night and I need some dough.' So round to the hotel I went, and out came Mr X carrying a sports bag and a hot water bottle. 'I want you to take me to the entrance of Hampstead Heath, which is at the top of Heath Street,' he said, 'then I want you to meet me by the Parliament Hill Fields exit, exactly two hours later.'

What on earth was he going to do in the middle of a cold winter's night on Hampstead Heath? I shuddered to think. It wasn't too long before I discovered the answer. We were at the traffic lights by Hampstead Station and the interior lights went on. I didn't take too much notice until a motorist came alongside and, with a broad grin on his face, beckoned me to look in the back of the cab. I turned round and thought, oh my God, I'm gonna get nicked for this. The geezer had taken all his clothes off and was putting on an old white singlet and a pair of those funny long running shorts they all wore in the popular film, *Chariots of Fire*. Thankfully, the lights went out while I proceeded up Heath Street chuckling away to myself. I thought I was going to keel over with laughter when he jumped out of the cab in his thirties running outfit. The picture of him running off into the darkness in the pouring rain will stay in my mind forever!

So it was back to home in Gospel Oak, a nice cup of tea and a sandwich and a read of the morning papers. And off I went again to pick him up at the bottom of Highgate West Hill. If the picture of him running off into the darkness was funny, then his eventual arrival after two hours of jogging in the thick mud nearly gave me a fit. I think it's probably the funniest thing I've ever seen in forty years of driving a London taxi. He was mud-spattered from head to foot and his spectacles looked like the goggles of a motorcyclist in a cross-country rally. He didn't say a word, just got back into the cab, switched the light on and started taking his muddy clothes off. I had a peek at him through the mirror and now realised why he carried a hot-water bottle. This was his mobile 'shower', and, with his flannel, he proceeded to wipe off the mud.

It must have been around 4 o'clock in the morning as we passed by my humble abode and I had had just about enough of this nutter for one night. I dropped him off at Belsize Park, copped my cheque, which, incidentally, doubled my night's takings, and made my way back home.

My deep sleep was interrupted by the sound of men's loud voices outside my bedroom window. They were talking about women and conquests and who was a 'raver' and who wasn't. That's strange, I thought to myself, still half asleep. How can I possibly hear men's voices outside my bedroom window, if I lived in a block of flats on the fourth floor. I opened the curtains and found the answer. Two men in a 'boat', busily cleaning all the windows! 'Do me a favour, guys,' I shouted out, 'I'm getting too excited listening to you and I can't sleep.'

The following Sunday, I decided to go out in the cab for a few hours because I had a golf tournament on the Monday. I think the time was around midday as I drove up Belsize Park. Yes, you've guessed it! Mr X called for a radio cab and I was right on top of the job. He dashed out as usual and this time wanted to go to the corner of Great Windmill Street and Brewer

Street in Soho. I knew from the cab grapevine that he was quite partial to a good working girl, so when he dashed off shouting 'Wait for me!', I knew it could be a long day. That, as it turned out, was the biggest understatement I've ever made.

I polished the cab from front to back. I read every Sunday paper I could find and I spent a small fortune in the well-known Salt Beef Bar, next to where I parked. But come 10 o'clock at night I'd had enough hanging around, so I called in on the radio for a willing relief. I was told afterwards that my relief stayed in the same spot until lunchtime the next day. When the other driver eventually got the cheque, it was nine hours' waiting for me and the rest for him. Believe me, sitting around for over nine hours, unable to move in case he came back at any time, was far harder than pushing a cab around London in heavy traffic!

As I stated before, Mr X had a penchant for the working girls and his particular favourite was a prostitute who worked around Soho, called Irish Mary. What extra services Irish Mary offered compared to the other girls, I'll never know. But Mr X enjoyed her company and employed a cab-driver mate of mine to pick her up most nights and bring her back to his hotel. My mate Lenny and Irish Mary worked out a scam that could benefit both of them financially. They agreed to graft all night on the pretence that Lenny couldn't find Mary. Then, around midnight, he would pick her up and take her to Belsize Park, saying to Mr X that she had been with punters all night.

So he would cop about seven hours' waiting time on top of his night's work and give Mary a 'drink' to keep her mouth shut. Mind you, Mary was on an earner as well. She had been grafting all evening and then had a punter waiting to see her through until the next morning.

Just before Mr X disappeared, as quickly as he had appeared, I picked him up for the last time, again late one night. As God is my witness, this is the truth. He came out of the hotel in the early hours of the morning, dressed completely in a cowboy outfit, even down to the two imitation guns in their holsters at his side. I didn't know whether to laugh or cry, this guy was losing it. But I was on good money, and if this caper turned him on, who was I to criticise? The same old drivel was coming from the back of the cab and the same boring instructions. 'We're heading for Smithfield Market, cabbie,' he said, 'and I want you to change into top gear by the time we reach England's Lane. Could you make doubly sure your speed is exactly twenty-seven miles an hour?' he continued, sitting back in his seat and studying his stop-watch.

You don't really need this after a hard night's work, I thought. But it will help pay for our next Spanish holiday! He directed me to the west side of Smithfield, just next to St Bartholomew's Church and behind the hospital. 'This is excellent, cabbie,' he shouted, jumping out of the taxi and running off into the night. 'Wait for me!' he shouted like a madman. 'I'm off to roam the prairie.'

He turned right into Cloth Fair, where the poet John

Betjeman lived at the time, and disappeared. This I simply had to see. So I got out of the cab and peered up Cloth Fair to have a quick peek. This guy was strutting up the alleyway with a cowboy-like gait, pulling out his guns and firing imaginary shots at the houses, then actually blowing into the barrels of the toy guns, before replacing them into their holsters with a twirl and a flourish. Suddenly, his Western dream got shattered. A crowd of rowdy Smithfield porters came walking down Cloth Fair, probably having just left the pub, and what they called Mr X is unrepeatable, in any shape or form. He made a run for it and I dashed back to the cab so he didn't see me peeking. 'Take me home immediately,' he puffed, 'this place is full of foul-mouthed yobs.' 'What's the problem, sir?' I asked innocently. 'The problem is, cabbie,' he replied tersely, 'that I was accosted by some louts.'

I drove him home and he seemed much more subdued than his normal self. Strangely enough, I felt sorry for the guy. He had all this dough, yet he was a lonely old man with a jumbled-up brain. I never saw Mr X again after that incident in Smithfield, and I never heard his name ever come over the radio. I've got a sneaky feeling his old ticker went following that scare and he keeled over soon afterwards. There'll never be another Mr X.

FIVE

THE ARRIVAL OF MINICABS

The private hire trade has always been accepted by the London cab trade as an acceptable part of the transport set-up. They tended to specialise in weddings, funerals and the supply of limos to high-flyers who required chauffeur-driven vehicles, while taxis concentrated on the short and immediate hirings on the streets of Central London. You will notice that I never use the euphemism that is popular in today's national press, 'Black Cab'. There is no such thing as a 'Black Cab'. There are only licensed taxis and unlicensed vehicles

Yet, on 19 June 1961, amid the ballyhoo whipped up by the press, a fleet of red Renault Dauphine minicabs, adorned with coloured ads and with the drivers wearing olive-green combat uniforms and matching soft hats, was launched on to the streets of London by Welbeck Motors. The man behind this venture was a Michael Gotla, who nurtured the idea and perfected it during the years he had run a legitimate hire car company. Mr Gotla had shrewdly realised that the old Private Hire laws had enough holes in them to enable him to drive even a Ford Granada through. The magic key to the success of the whole venture was the pre-booking of every vehicle. If his cars had two-way radios and a well-trained staff on the phone lines, then he reckoned he could run a full-blown taxi service by the back door, without the overheads of stringent Hackney Carriage laws, costly custom-built taxis and annual overhauls.

But he needed capital to start his grand plan and he finally got this in 1959 from Isaac Wolfson's General Guarantee Company, who backed his venture by acquiring for £15,000 a 51 per cent controlling interest in Welbeck Motors, to whom it then proceeded to lend a massive £1 million. The services of a couple of MPs were needed to bring an air of respectability to the venture and their job was to soften up the public. They were to ask questions like, 'London's cabs are unable to meet the needs of the public and I suggest the introduction of minicabs and motorised rickshaws which would require Home Office approval.'

This question was asked seven months before the first red Renault Dauphines took to the streets. These MPs got a blank from the Government when Mr Denis Vosper, Minister of State at the Home Office, replied, 'There are three arguments against their use. They will not be strong enough to stand the wear and tear as the average yearly mileage of a London taxi is 40,000. They have been tried, in 1928, but there was no demand for them; and the limited demand now will not justify their manufacture.'

Having failed to gain the Government's open approval, they turned their campaign to a more receptive channel, the press. *The Times* of 2 March 1961 reported: 'Men of wealth have been heard to cry out against the taximeter – men who think nothing of signing away many thousands in seconds in a wiggle of a pen, but find it very painful to sit helplessly in the back of a taxi watching their money dripping away in threepenny stages.'

The writer in *The Times* seemed blissfully unaware of the fact that some sixty years previously, his paper had been in the van of the campaign for the introduction of the taximeter!

So the red Renaults hit the London streets in 1961 and Gotla's slogan was 'A shilling a mile, anywhere, anytime'. Most experienced cabmen realised at the time that these fares were unrealistic and only a kick-off price. The Home Office, washed their hands of the whole matter, sharing the Government's view that minicabs were an extension of the private hire car trade and as such, were to be welcomed. The Government, in its wisdom, regarded the existing law as adequate to protect the licensed taxi trade. But, as events unfolded, it became obvious that there were those who were determined to see that the law was abused. The Government continually stated that, as plying for hire had no statutory definition, it was difficult to obtain any convictions. Yet they and previous governments had had ample time to study the Hindley Report of 1939 and the Runciman Report of 1953, that defined plying for hire by law.

Gotla had planned his strategy well and, even though there were ugly confrontations with cabmen and strikes and legal actions, Welbeck Motors continued getting front-page publicity. But the crux of the matter was that Welbeck Motors couldn't make a profit and in 1962, the following statement appeared in *The Times*: 'The General Guarantee Company has today sold its 51 per cent interest in Welbeck Motors to Mr R.S. Walker. Mr Gotla has also sold his 25 per cent interest to Mr Walker and has resigned as Managing Director.'

It was heavily rumoured at the time that Mr Isaac Wolfson, as he then was, had been told that the controversy surrounding his minicab venture could cost him his coveted knighthood. Not long after selling his shares in Welbeck, he did indeed receive his knighthood and, as Sir Isaac Wolfson, became famous for his philanthropy. He died in 1991.

Everyone knew the company had financial problems, but the final demise of Welbeck Motors was not to occur until 1965, when the company faced a petition for its compulsory winding-up. The petition had been brought by the City of Westminster for rates amounting to £2,652 and the Inland Revenue who were owned £8,750 and a total liability of £50,000. An order was made for the winding up of the company.

One MP who had lobbied for Gotla was left stranded in the chamber when Gotla and his financial backers departed from the scene. All he could do now to hide his embarrassment was to make fun of the situation, saying: 'It is high time the winds of change blew through the Public Carriage Office, it was festooned with cobwebs, strewn with horse manure and had an all-pervading smell of horses. The London cab trade wanted a monopoly and a scarcity of cabs.' The MP needed to get his facts right. He knew full well that the Public Carriage Office only implemented the law, they didn't make it. He also knew that there is no limitation on cabs or drivers in London, only an economic limiting factor. Taxis increase when it is financially viable to do so, in exactly the same way that other forms of private enterprise increase. The taxi trade has a disadvantage that other businesses do not have, its income is strictly limited by Parliament.

Unfortunately, the end of Welbeck Motors wasn't the end of the minicab scourge, it was just the beginning and the opening of the floodgates. Gotla had shown there was a loophole in the Private Hire laws and that loophole was still there to exploit. Again, with the benefit of hindsight, the cab trade could have stopped Gotla before he'd even got off the ground. The all-powerful TGWU could easily have instructed their dockers to black the Renault Dauphines coming in from France and not to unload them. But they didn't, for whatever reason, much to the regret of every future London cabbie.

Many shrewd and powerful people were sitting, carefully watching in the wings, while the Welbeck scenario reached its inevitable conclusion. The game plan had been shown to them. All they had to do when they chose to enter the ball-game, was to get their strategy and figures correct to ensure maximum profits.

MINICABS PROLIFERATE

Despite successful court cases brought by the TGWU and the Crisis Committee over the definition of 'Plying For Hire', and the banning of self-advertising on minicabs, the unlicensed opposition seemed to be increasing alarmingly every year. Simply anyone could become a minicab driver, the operations were mostly unlicensed and there were no legally enforced checks on the vehicles or the drivers: anyone could start up as a minicab service, all they needed was a car.

Meanwhile, what was the powerful – but not totally united – cab trade doing about the interlopers? Well, not a lot, to be quite honest. Mind you, they had formed a new organisation in the seventies called the LTDA, the Licensed Taxi Drivers Association, because many cabbies thought the TGWU was far too political. I'll forever remember the inaugural meeting of the LTDA at the Central Hall, Westminster. There were rousing and passionate speeches from the platform, informing the cabbies that this ginger group was formed with one specific purpose in mind – and I quote – 'Of ridding the streets of London from the minicab scourge'. Sadly, like many other ginger groups set up as viable alternatives to unions, they didn't succeed with their one specific purpose. As the years rolled by, they did succeed in becoming the biggest organisation in the cab trade. They diversified and started a radio circuit, which now is among the largest in London. Then an excellent Sick Scheme, a Credit Union and many more good things were introduced for their members. But unfortunately, along the way, they lost their way. They became a flourishing business providing long-term and secure, well-paid jobs for the ex-taxi-drivers on their Executive. I'm not knocking getting paid the rate for the job, but what a difference from when we first started in our dilapidated offices in the Edgware Road. Everyone chipped in, and all for love. Sadly, their one specific purpose for being formed in the first instance, and the reason for all those rousing and passionate speeches in the seventies, got lost in the process.

As for the vast majority of London cabbies in the sixties and the seventies, myself included, we sat around in cab shelters just talking tough and doing nowt! The trade organised many protests against the unfair competition, which included a very successful 'Drive-in' to the County Hall private car park, and two or three 'Drive-ins' around Piccadilly and Parliament Square. The co-ordinated 'Rest Day', when cabbies were asked not to go to work, was particularly well supported. But, at the end of the day, it was the minicab companies themselves who were benefiting from all of our stoppages. They were earning loads of money with hardly any cabs on the streets of London

– except for the 'scab-cabs', who did not join in. The government of the day simply ignored our pleas for a change in the law.

I believe the trade's finest united hour in my long experience was in the late seventies. For some unknown reason, we had been denied our annual cost of living increase for the previous three years. Both garages and cabbies were feeling the pinch as prices started rising. So one Sunday afternoon late in 1978, the trade organised a drive-in to Whitehall, in an attempt to gain public sympathy for our plight. It truly was a wonderful sight to see the cabbies and their families driving down London's most prestigious street in the bright sunshine. Then, after meetings with the police, the taxis were parked from Trafalgar Square all the way down to Parliament Square and the street was blocked off. I remember thinking at the time, we are all pleading poverty, but the cabbies and our wives and children are all beautifully dressed and turned out, we look positively affluent!

After some rousing speeches from our leaders, a deputation from the trade was allowed to present a petition to Number 10 Downing Street. I had the honour of presenting it in person, by virtue of the fact that I was still Taxi-Driver of the Year, after winning the annual competition the previous month. In those days, there were no massive gates protecting Downing Street and our supporters were lined ten deep on each side, all shouting and cheering. I'm sure our drive-in worked, because in the following April, we received a massive 25 per cent increase that lost us many fares, due to the fact that it was too big an increase at one time.

As with the speedy conversion from horses to motor cabs, the minicab trade blossomed alarmingly. Within a few short years the suburbs, because of the lack of cabs, became their stronghold. Next they started to spread to South London, and that's when the apathy in the cab trade manifested itself. Apart from a group of caring cabbies setting up the Walworth Road Booking Service as a viable opposition to the minicabs, opposition was minimal; incidentally, they went broke for lack of support. It was always the same story whenever you spoke to cabmen and tried to convince them that this minicab menace was a real threat to their livelihood. They seemed to believe because they'd done the Knowledge, the coveted Green Badge was sacrosanct and they had a right to a monopoly on the streets of London. Their favourite saying was 'There will always be a need for taxis in London and we'll always be able to get a living'. And for sure, you will always be able to get a living driving a cab in London. But how many hours will you have to do in the future to achieve this living?

Consequently, within a few short years, we had meekly surrendered the whole of South London to the scruffy minicab offices in every High Street. Even the normally very busy and popular cab ranks with telephones at Camberwell Green and Clapham Common were vacated by drivers who had worked the same rank for years, all because of the lack of work coming from walk-ups and the telephone. This situation was partly our fault. Many cabbies simply refused to go south and cross any of the bridges for fear of a 'nose bleed', so the punters relied on the minicabs, who were happy to go anywhere at any time. The busy phone ranks in Central London soon fell into disuse. The once very busy taxi rank at Shepherds Bush was used by dozens of regular drivers, who were quite happy to keep going up the Uxbridge Road, then back to the rank. Suddenly the radio circuits started using it as a calling point for the TV Centre in Wood Lane, because many of the radio men were 'hanging it up' outside waiting for a 'cream fare'. So, when one of the regular customers rang up for a local taxi, many radio men would say, 'I'll be round in a couple of minutes.' After putting the phone down, they would say to the cabbie who was second on the rank that somebody wanted to book a cab for the next day. This went on continually for weeks and weeks, until eventually the regular customers started ringing for a minicab as being the more reliable option.

The selfsame fate befell the very popular George Rank on Haverstock Hill. Very often, between 8 and 9 in the morning, there would be fifteen or twenty cabs ranked up waiting for the phone to ring. It was so busy, you could expect to get off in ten minutes or so. Not just local rides into the City or the West End, I got countless fares to Heathrow and Gatwick and all over the place off the George. But unfortunately the non-regulars on the rank would see the phone light flashing as they cruised down Haverstock Hill, pick up the phone, and if the destination didn't suit them they didn't bother to turn up. The phones themselves were often sabotaged. So, within a short space of time, one of the busiest ranks in London had bitten the dust and all the regulars, myself included, headed for the West End and the orbit up and down Oxford Street! The same fate befell many other once busy cab ranks.

The minicabs next got a foothold in North London, again with the help of the cab trade itself. Most of the licensed radio circuits had a policy of not picking up outside phone boxes, pubs or Irish dance halls. It was a common sight to see empty cabs with their 'For Hire' signs switched off, driving down Kilburn High Road late at night, completely ignoring the frantic waves of droves of Irish merrymakers wanting a taxi. In fact, any cabbies known to work the predominantly Irish area of 'County Kilburn' were looked upon as nutters! I was one of those so-called nutters, but I stuck strictly to my game plan: the safest fares were those who had a girl with them. Even if he was slightly the worse for wear, the man would probably have a kiss and a cuddle in the back and be no trouble. Long before the Aussies arrived to colonise Earls Court in the sixties and seventies the Paddies had already started the trend of not tipping. But the cabbies weren't too bothered, they just stuck a couple of bob more on the extras. While on the subject of the extras (night charge, extra passengers, luggage, etc.), that reminds of a hilarious discussion I had with a boozy Paddy and his lady friend one St Patrick's Night. We arrived at his destination and he got out to pay me off.

'That'll be two quid including the extras, my old mate,' I said in a friendly manner. 'Could I be asking you a question, surr?' he replied. 'Of course you can, mate, just fire away and I'll do my best to answer,' said I. 'Well,' he asked, looking at the taximeter, 'how does that there meter know when it's gone midnight and it's time for the night charge? And,' he went on, 'how the divil does it know another person is getting into the taxi?'

It's not very often I'm at a loss for words, but this was one of them. I didn't have the heart to tell him it's the cabbie who hits the extras button, so I mumbled something about the wonders of modern technology!

Another night I was coming down Kilburn Road and, as I pulled up alongside another cab, I noticed a geezer in the back on his knees, seemingly talking to himself.

'What's up with him, mate?' I shouted across to the other cabbie. 'Oh, don't take any notice of him,' he replied, with a big grin on his face, 'he's boozed out of his mind and talking a load of rubbish, so I told him to kneel down and talk into the microphone so I could hear him better!'

I chuckled to myself as I pulled away. I bet the poor old Paddy didn't get much response from the heater outlet! We all do silly things when we've had too much to drink, but the Irish tend to do strange things when they've not had a drink. Now don't get me wrong, I love the Irish, but they do make me giggle. Take the case of an Irish cabbie mate of mine, telling me a story. He dropped off this huge drunken Paddy in the middle of a winter's night with snow and hail lashing down, around the back of the White City Stadium, near to Queens Park Rangers Ground.

'So,' says this huge Paddy, lurching in the back of the cab like a stranded whale, 'what will you be a-doing if oi don't pay the fare?' 'Well,' said my mate John, putting on a strong Irish accent, even though he was born in London, 'I don't want one of my fellow countrymen to get into any trouble with the police.'

The huge Paddy sat in the back for a moment, trying to get his befuddled brain into working mode. Then he says, 'Oi'll tell you what oi'll do. Oi'll race you to the top of the road for double or nothing.'

I'm just sitting there laughing my head off and imagining the funny scene, and I said to John, 'So, what d'ya do, John, dump him round the nick?' 'Not so likely,' replied John. 'I knew he was well drunk and wouldn't last fifty yards. So I took off my jacket, locked it in the cab and we started the race,' said John with a smile.

I couldn't believe what I was hearing and I had to say to him in total disbelief, 'Yeah, but it was snowing and the middle of a winter's night, for Christ's sake.' 'You may think us Irish are thick,' he laughed, 'but I won the race and got double the fare, so who's the thick one?'

You got the odd runner or bilker working the 'Paddy Fields' and one night I picked him up at Cricklewood for just a short fare round the corner to Willesden. He asked me to stop, then shot out of the back door like a greyhound out of the trap. Now the regular bilker normally sorts out an alleyway between two houses as his bolt-hole. Not this guy, a typical Paddy. He'd done a runner directly outside his lodgings and I'd even seen him go in the front door. I sat outside a minute and, as God is my witness, a light went on upstairs and his face appeared at the window waving at me. If I'd called the police and got him nicked, it would have cost me the best part of a night's work for the sake of a few bob. So I just waved back at him, bursting my sides with laughter and drove off!

Because of the lack of coverage by taxis in these areas, in a very short space of time dozens of minicab offices opened up adjacent to all the many Irish dance halls in Kilburn, Willesden, Camden Town, Cricklewood and the Archway. They did a roaring trade every night of the week at the expense of the cab trade, but the cab trade simply ignored the facts. Consequently, when these passengers wanted transport at any other time, quite rightly they chose to phone a minicab because they were the only ones who were willing to take them home a bit boozy. It's very difficult for the new cabbies to comprehend, but when places like the Buffalo Club in Camden Town or the Galtymore up in Cricklewood turned out, there were literally hundreds of people wanting taxis. There were also plenty of police wagons ready to pick up the drunks and I've seen them throw the Paddies in head first and heard the bang and the scream as they hit the deck!

In a very short space of time it became almost a knock-on effect. The minicabs prospered on our rejected fares, which gave them a regular customer base to build on and eventually expand their business into legitimate account work. As for the nightmen who used to work the Irish dance halls, well, they are probably now orbiting the West End with all the other cabs, many who maybe regularly worked the defunct South and North London ranks! The cake is only so big and if lots of people start taking a slice, then it doesn't leave much, does it?

Once the minicab floodgates burst open, the cake got almost eaten and the cab trade's area of influence became smaller and smaller. We got accustomed to just working the City, the West End, Chelsea, Kensington, Bayswater and Hampstead. But, lately, even these areas – especially Soho and the City – are being threatened by a new breed of minicab driver, the minicab tout. He is not attached to any company at all and will steal a fare at any time, or at any place. The West End is infested with these touts who blatantly pick up in front of empty taxis. My friends who still work nights tell me that things are getting completely out of hand and that Soho is now a no-go area for licensed taxis! Even the clubs in the City have touts waiting outside to offer their illegal services. When our trade organisations complain to the police about the activities of the touts, they tell us they are undermanned and touting is considered a low priority. Yet the legislation is already in place giving them powers to arrest these touts!

It will be interesting to see what happens in the future now that minicabs – or Private Hire Vehicles (PHVs) – have been licensed. At the time of writing this book, 1,600 minicab companies had been sent a licensing form that needed to be completed and returned by August 2001 and a massive 40,000 'minicabbies' were waiting to have their cars inspected by the PCO.

The major PHV companies will need all their drivers to have the proper Passenger Liability Insurance and evidence they are not also claiming Jobseeker's Allowance or other benefits. The cars will require a thorough MOT twice a year and their licensing will be strictly enforced by the Public Carriage Office. Whether these extra overheads will cause them to raise their prices and result in a more level playing field remains to be seen. This present legislation will certainly rid London of the majority of back street minicab offices but whether it gets rid of the touts is another matter. Only persistence by the police and local councils can achieve that.

I don't think our right to ply for hire will be challenged for many years to come. But, mark my words, it will be eventually. As I perceive the future of our trade, the biggest threat from the newly-licensed PHVs in Central London will be directed at the licensed radio circuits. For many years the old minicabs were considered by the big corporate companies in the City as a little bit seedy. Yes, okay to run the staff or middle management home, but certainly not one of the big bosses. That's all changed now they are licensed. That licence gives them not only an air of respectability, it also gives them credibility, which is what they were looking for.

Playing devil's advocate is a good way of working out what the opposition is thinking. Their next obvious step would be to approach the big corporates and undercut the present prices they pay for their accounts with the licensed radio circuits and, unfortunately, they *can* undercut the present prices with their smaller overheads. If over a period of years they manage to secure the major accounts, then we could be in big trouble. I believe there are around 6,000 cabbies on the four radio circuits and many of those 6,000 cabbies may well come off the circuits owing to lack of work and join the orbit up and down Oxford Street. They could be joined, if the PHVs succeed in cutting off our client base at Heathrow with a successful booking service, by another 2,000-plus cabbies, all doing the same orbit. And don't forget the many hotels in Central London. The bosses at head office may well favourably consider any offer from a licensed PHV company to purchase a franchise on their guests' personal transport requirements. So, sitting on hotel ranks hoping somebody will eventually come out and say the magic words that bring a smile to your face, like 'Heathrow please, driver', may be a thing of the past.

Many cabbies have nicknamed me 'Doom and Gloom' because of some of my prophecies for the trade. But you just can't live forever in cloud-cuckoo-land and pretend that nothing detrimental is happening to your living. The world doesn't owe us a living simply because we chose to do the Demon Knowledge. Even that looks like being streamlined in the near future if certain vested interests get their way. Then the Knowledge could well become a watered-down version that even an idiot could pass, thus diluting our professional and world-renowned image.

For sure, my prophecies can be construed by many as purely hypothetical, especially by some cabbies who don't want to look any farther than the next fare. I must confess that I do worry about the attitude of many of the new drivers coming into the trade. Quite honestly, some of them don't give a damn, whereas we were always fearful about 'doing our Bill' (losing our cab licences for being naughty boys). But the facts speak for themselves, and it's up to us to get our act together, because if we don't then we certainly won't last another 300 years!

SIX

THE HEATHROW STORY

The foundations of Heathrow's place in history were laid 25 million years ago when south-east England became submerged under the sea. A flat layer of gravel was deposited 14 miles west of what is now Trafalgar Square, and it was this flatness and the excellent drainage characteristics of the gravel that made Heathrow the perfect site for an airport.

Man's place in the Heathrow landscape has been traced back to a Celtic-Roman temple excavated in 1944. Pottery discovered on the site dates from 300 BC. In Roman times, Hounslow Heath was forested land through which a Roman road ran from London to what is now Staines, and then on to the West Country.

In the thirteenth century, Henry III cleared the forest, thereby creating the heath, on which grew a hamlet variously known in subsequent centuries as 'Hetherewe', 'Hetherow', 'Hedrowe' and 'Heath Row'. By the seventeenth century, the muddy and difficult road across the open heathland, much used by stagecoaches travelling in and out of London, became the haunt of highwaymen. The most famous of them all, a woman called Molly Cutpurse, was the leader of a gang of audacious robbers, many of whom were executed at Tyburn Tree, a public gallows close to where Marble Arch now stands. Their remains were then brought back to Hounslow Heath and hung on gibbets as a deterrent to others. Legend has it that the site was also frequented by Dick Turpin, who is said to have hidden from the law behind a fireplace in the Green Man pub at Hatton. By the eighteenth century, the area was used by gentlemen duellists to settle their quarrels and later by the army for drills, exercises and parades.

The earliest written reference to Heathrow is found on a 1749 map which refers to a small hamlet on the site of which is now Terminal Three, as 'Hitherow'. In 1784, the flatness of Heathrow and its proximity to London and the Royal Observatory of Greenwich, made it the perfect site for the original base mark of the world's very first Ordnance Survey. Major General William Roy and his troops hammered in wooden pikes at Heathrow, and again at the poor house at Hampton Hill in the south. His second line from Hangar Hill, Ealing to the east went through his first line and on to St Anne's Hill, Chertsey in the west. And from these two lines, he not only made up the first two triangles of England's very first Ordnance Survey; he also began the first international system, that was to reach across to France and on to the farthest corners of the earth.

The original wooden pike at Heathrow was replaced

by an upright cannon, which was moved to the site of the old Taxi Feeder Park in 1944 during the airport's construction. Hence the name of our old canteen, 'General Roy's'.

Heathrow's place in aviation history can be traced back to the First World War when the army used nearby Hounslow Heath as a training aerodrome for the Royal Fighting Corps. In response to Zeppelin bombers, a crescent of aerodromes was built around the south of London, of which Hounslow Heath became the HQ. After the war it remained a military airfield until 1919, when it became the first 'customs' airport for London. In the 1920s, Hounslow Heath lost its early lead in civil aviation to Croydon. But during the Second World War a search began for a military aerodrome suitable for long-term expansion, able to function as the supply base for Tiger Force, the RAF's striking force for the Far East War, and also capable of handling the new longer-range military transport aircraft.

Pressure was also mounting to find a new site for the future civil airport for London. Croydon was considered inappropriate for future expansion because it was built on a hill and surrounded by urban sprawl. The decision was made to develop the 'Heath Row' site as a main terminal airport, with its initial use by RAF Transport Command. At the end of 1943, a Cabinet Committee took the decision that London's new airport after the war should be Heathrow. Speaking about the decision, Lord Winster, the Civil Aviation Minister, said:

The site is only 12 miles from the centre of

London. The land is remarkably level and the gravel sub-soil has excellent bearing and drainage qualities. To meet the need for a major airport to serve London, 52 sites were surveyed. No better site to the purpose could be found than Heathrow. One of the reasons that led to the excellence of the London Airport in this district was that it could be done with the minimum disturbance to householders.

At that time Heathrow was surrounded by market gardens.

On 31 May 1944, a Compulsory Purchase Order was drawn up by the Government and, using emergency wartime powers, the Air Ministry acquired 2,800 acres, excluding the original Hounslow Heath 'customs' and military airfield, but including the hamlet, Heath Row, and the Great West Aerodrome. On 6 June work began on the runways. Aircraft are required to take off into the prevailing wind and an RAF triangular pattern of runways was adopted to allow take-offs in any wind direction. A committee later decided to develop the original pattern into a Star of David, or double-triangle, to allow parallel take-offs and landings in any wind direction. The formal title, 'London Airport Heathrow', was adopted from 25 March 1946. The very first aircraft to land at the new airport was a BOAC Lancastrian from Australia, quickly followed by Lockheed Constellation airliners of Pan American and American Overseas Airways.

The emphasis on runways rather than terminal capacity led to the creation of a temporary tent village on the north side of the airfield. A row of red telephone boxes and a mobile post office stood alongside the tents. The tents were furnished with comfortable chintz armchairs, with a bar, a W.H. Smith & Son, a Cable and Wireless desk and Elsan toilets.

How different Heathrow is today. It's the busiest international airport in the world, with four terminals – soon to be five. It handles around 55 million passengers every year, almost equivalent to the entire population of the United Kingdom! And did you know it sells 26,000 cups of tea and coffee, 6,500 pints of beer and 6,500 sandwiches to the public every day of the year?

HEATHROW CABBIES

The London cab trade has traditionally provided passengers at Heathrow Airport with an excellent, personalised transport service for almost half a century. It's true to say that in the bad old days, the flow of taxis at Heathrow relied on the whims and vested interests of small groups of cabbies who organised themselves into cartels, or gangs. If my memory serves me right, I believe one 'firm' was called the Quality Street Gang and the other was the Lavender Hill Mob. If you didn't belong to one of these gangs, you simply couldn't get on a rank: when one cab got off, they would simply leave a space in the middle, only pulling forward when one of their gang appeared.

Consequently, all the Connaughts (Connaught Rangers – strangers) were forced to continually orbit, that is, circle the three terminal ranks hoping to find a space. It was obvious to all that an international airport like Heathrow couldn't possibly function in a professional way with a taxi operation like the one then in place. Especially after some bitter complaints from very influential people, not least the late Bobby Kennedy, brother of the President and Attorney General of the United States. His official limo had failed to turn up one Sunday morning while he was in transit at Heathrow. As a practising Catholic, he wanted to go to Mass at a local church in Hounslow, but not a single cab was prepared to take him, probably because it was only a short ride. This major complaint, coupled with many more, had the effect of forcing the BAA urgently to sort out a fair and sensible taxi operation. Their first attempt at using what is now the Bus Depot in the Central Area as a taxi-feeder rank was unsuccessful because it wasn't big enough. Finally, they utilised some spare space out on the Northern Perimeter Road, bang opposite the Heathrow Police Station.

That's when the trouble – and the eventual strikes – started. The BAA informed the trade organisations that they would be levying an entrance charge on each taxi using the new Feeder Park. Even though the suggested original charge was only a nominal 50p, the drivers and their organisations were furious, telling the BAA in no uncertain manner that they supplied a service for *their* passengers, who had already paid exorbitant landing charges for the privilege of arriving at Heathrow. Many of the wiser old heads realised that a nominal 50p might well be the thin end of the wedge, with the possibility of an increase every year. How right they were. The present entry fee, at the time of writing this book, is now a whopping £2.40 per cab, with a minimum purchase of ten credits: that's £24!

The battle lines were drawn, with neither side even willing to compromise or negotiate. The cabbies were adamant: withdraw the charge, or they would withdraw their labour. And so the strike began, with various volunteers, mostly TGWU members, picketing the entrance to the new feeder park. The support from the drivers was almost total, with just a few scabs ignoring the pickets. After seven weeks or so and with a Judicial Review about to be heard, with a possible result going our way, the drivers received a body blow from within. The General Secretary of one of the biggest trade organisations stated that he would be instructing his members to use the new feeder park facility, whatever the outcome of the Judicial Review. That was enough to make the men think long and hard about the future. What was the point of continuing if thousands of cabbies were going to drive through? The strike crumbled, and after some nine long weeks the BAA had won. With the benefit of hindsight, I think we could have won if we had held out for another couple of weeks. The BAA had been receiving bundles of complaints from influential passengers about the lack of taxis and questions were being asked in the House. The BAA were definitely wobbling and they might well have decided to cut and run within a few days or so.

Over a period of years, the BAA installed a workable system in the Taxi Feeder Park that catered for more than 400 taxis. But in 1998 we were told we had to move to a new, custom-built site, because the present land we occupied was prime real estate near the tunnel entrance. As a Trade Rep at the time, I was invited to a site meeting to offer my comments with the others. But, unfortunately, like most other BAA negotiations with our trade, the whole meeting was a complete sham. We honestly and foolishly believed that our input and suggestions would be acted upon, only to find out later that the plans had already been approved by BAA Management and this so-called site meeting was nothing more than a talking shop and PR exercise for the BAA.

After much useless negotiation, with the BAA apparently ignoring every single suggestion we put forward and things going wrong as we predicted, we finally moved to a fully computerised site, complete with new canteen and new toilets and two feeder parks with a total capacity of almost 500. But who would pay for the brand-new computers, the extra Traffic Wardens required and the extra cleaning staff to sweep the feeder parks? That's only meant to be a rhetorical question, because certainly the BAA wasn't going to pay!

THE SYSTEM AND THE ABUSES

Any full computerised system in this day and age should be fully reliable and idiot-proof. Not so with a small minority of devious London cabbies. They could break out of Alcatraz or Colditz if needs be! What could be easier? You drive into the Northern Feeder Park, with each row holding around a dozen cabs or more. When the row next to you moves out you then follow the cab in front, cross over the road to the Southern Feeder Park and eventually pass the Entry reader that registers your badge number, the number of credits you've got left and the number of the group you need to park in. When your group eventually moves out towards the exit reader, after waiting up to two hours or so if it's slow, the exit reader instructs you which terminal to go to, One, Two, Three or Four. When arriving at your designated terminal, the Traffic Wardens in control of that rank should, in a purely literal sense, ask for your badge number and check it out on their computer print-outs. All very straightforward enough and all very professional.

But here's the rub. If, as over the last couple of years, these Heathrow Traffic Wardens have had a running disagreement with their Metropolitan Police boss, who has insisted on a cut-back in staff manning the taxi ranks at Heathrow, then it becomes far from straightforward and very unprofessional. They have argued that just one warden on each rank cannot do the job of asking all destinations, as well as checking badge numbers. And, in their wisdom, they haven't been checking badge numbers to verify that each cab on the rank has been through the system legally. So, in one fell swoop, their action has negated the whole tried and tested system and made the vastly expensive computer and its software completely useless. Now the honest cabbies at Heathrow are reaping the crooked crop sown by the wardens in their haste to involve our trade in their internal dispute!

It's become open house on the terminal ranks at the time of writing this book, and the devious cabbies are plucking a fair share of that crop. With the help of mobile phones and friends down on the terminals, the devious cabbies swoop like vultures when they get the call that no badge numbers are being taken. The fact that their mates in the feeder park are having to wait another half-hour or so because they are stealing the fares doesn't concern these scallywags one iota. They have only one concern and that's attempting to nick as many fares in the day as humanly possible. To date, nothing has changed for over two years, despite the fact that the BAA and HALT are probably losing an annual revenue on the taxi entry charge in the region of £30,000. I doubt if anything will change until the wardens succeed in their battle against their bosses but at the cabbies' and their employer's expense!

In the absence of full-time supervision, a small number of cabbies have perfected various scams, such as covering their computerised Cabtags with silver paper so it doesn't register when you first enter the feeder park. Then, after waiting just a short while, they follow the next group out and, after getting a

'Go To Control' on the exit reader, go back up to the warden's cabin to convince them that the entry reader was faulty and not recording some cabs. They are then issued with a ticket for the terminal of their choice and, hey presto, have saved maybe two hours waiting and £2.40 on the entry charge! Then you had – and still have – the scam on the radio ranks. These ranks were installed for the sole use of radio drivers picking up pre-booked account fares and it took months of hard negotiating before the idea was accepted by the BAA on a trial basis. So their future is tenuous to say the least. Yet the bad boys persist in using them to steal fares, in full view of their friends on the main rank. The drivers know their names, as do the wardens, the police and the BAA. Yet the same faces operate the same scams every day without getting nicked. Which poses the pertinent question, why? Well, for a start, the London cabbie has this strong feeling of camaraderie with his fellow drivers and their unwritten code is 'You never shop one of your own'. This is fine in the broad aspect of the job and should be admired. But the scallywags are blatantly stealing from their fellow drivers – yet they stroll around the canteen admired by all, almost like modern-day Robin Hoods. But they ain't robbing the rich!

So even though the regulars moan like mad, the 'cabbie's code', mixed with a fair amount of apathy, means the various scams, coupled with the wardens' ineptitude, will always continue to plague Heathrow until the authorities finally decide to get a grip on the situation. If I were a BAA shareholder, I would make myself heard at the AGM and ask why the company was losing so much revenue in the Taxi Feeder Park.

However, around the time of this book's publication in 2003 it appears that most wardens are doing their jobs properly.

REGULARS AND THEIR NICKNAMES

When passengers arrive at any one of the four terminals and see a dozen taxis or more on each rank, they wrongly assume that these dozen taxis are the entire complement on the airport. Yet if they were to pop over to the Northern Perimeter Road, they'd be in for a big shock. The taxi operation at Heathrow is massive, with some 3,000 cab movements on a busy day and the two feeder parks, with a capacity of nearly 500, filling and emptying four or five times over an 18-hour period. And as for the canteen, well, when it's full it's not unlike the Parrot House at the London Zoo, because cabbies tend to shout when they talk. Almost every airport regular has a mobile phone, for obvious business reasons, and when they all start ringing in the canteen, it's like a BT Telephone Exchange!

Individually, the Heathrow regular is a pleasant enough person, but collectively they can become aggressive and volatile. I think this stems from the past when all the 'town drivers' resented their cartels and gangs and looked upon them as 'villains'. So now the airport regulars tend to stick together and look after their own. The generous collections they regularly make for their sick friends and charities on the entry gate are legend throughout the trade. Many's the time I've seen a black book going around the canteen for an extra collection for a very sick mate. You just give a fiver, or a tenner, and sign your name in the book, quite often on a weekly basis. Strangely enough, the airport regulars are not considered as 'villains' when 'town drivers' come out to apply for a 'list' (a collection on the gate) for one of their sick mates, who has maybe never ever 'put on' at Heathrow!

The airport regular is as sharp as a razor, with a wicked sense of humour. You are given a nickname early on, for a variety of reasons. Maybe it's where you live: 'Bagshot' Bill, 'Hounslow' Ted, or maybe 'Ashford' 'Arry. Or maybe it's your physical features, like 'Banana Nose', or 'Wing-Nuts', ears that stick out a bit, or 'Flipper', with the dodgy feet, or even Lenny 'Shoulders', or Ted 'The Neck'. I got lumbered with Alf 'The Pipe', or, because of my journalism connections, often it was 'Scoop'. Maybe it could even be your attire that gives you the nickname, like 'Woolly Hat' George, or John 'The Hat', or Fred 'The Suit'. Then you had the guys who looked somewhat like the actors on the TV, like 'The Milky Bar Kid', or 'Emmerdale', or 'Brains', as in *Thunderbirds*, the 'Muppet', or 'Joe 90', or 'Emu'. Then there's a Perry 'Kettles' who mends watches. 'Kettle' is old Cockney rhyming slang for 'kettle and hob' (fob watch). Where your parents originated from is another source of nicknames: there's Mick 'The Greek' and George 'The Greek', 'Italian' Tony and 'Italian' Vic, 'Scotch' John,

'Welsh' Bob and 'Manchester' Ted. Even your previous job conjures up a nickname with Fred 'The Fireman', Ron 'The Dust' – as in dustman, the 'Coalman', Danny 'The Docker' and 'Postman' Pat and Sid 'The Grocer'. We even have 'Sheepdog' (shaggy hair and beard) and, in the old days, 'The Jolly Green Giant'. Then your driving warrants a nickname at Heathrow. You've got the guy who bombs it all the time, Chrissy 'Hot Wheels'. Then the way you eat or your particular eating habits: 'Knives and Forks' is eating all the time, while 'Bread Roll' Mick has a bread roll with everything. Many of the nicknames are rather crude, and not to be mentioned in this book. But one of my particular favourites, and a really nice guy, is this fella who can never back a winner, never gets a good fare and never wins at cards. Everyone knows 'Sufferin' Peter! Again, what fascinates me is where some of these guys live. I did a little survey recently to find out which Heathrow cabbie lives the farthest away from the airport. Towns along the South Coast don't even rate in the top ten. Nor does Somerset, Devon, Cornwall, or even Wales and Scotland. We're talking foreign parts here! Quite a few live in Spain and Portugal and elsewhere on the Continent. I thought I'd found a winner when someone told me about 'Maltese' Arthur. Arthur does two months in London and the next two months or more at his Maltese home. But then I heard on the grapevine about 'American' John, who had to be the winner. John has got a place in West Palm Beach, Florida, and does six months here and six months there! Many of these cabbies who live thousands of miles away tend to live with relatives close to the airport and some just sleep in their cabs. One of the best known of the 'sleepers' is 'Mr Pastry'. Legend has it that he actually used to cook his breakfast on a primus stove in the back of his cab!

Many of these hard-core, regular Heathrow cabbies never work in 'town'. They wait their turn, sometimes as long as three hours. They do their 'ride' into town, turn round and come back again. It's certainly not about earning lots of dosh that they work in this manner, they would earn more in the West End. It's all about relaxing and the quality of life. They have a good meal in the canteen, a game of cards and a chat with their mates and, if they are feeling particularly energetic, they can stand in the summer sunshine cleaning and polishing their cabs. But, the bottom line is they don't have to face the West End traffic chaos for eight hours or more every day. And, when you've been driving a London taxi for some forty years, as in my case and in the case of many of the Heathrow regulars, you just want an easy life with no hassle.

I love listening to some of the funny – sometimes tragic – tales told in the canteen. Take the case of 'Hampstead' Brian, who took a guy all the way to Leeds a few years back. By the time they reached Leeds it was dark and the guy suddenly stabbed Brian in the back of the neck and ran off. Thankfully Brian recovered, but they never found his assailant. On a lighter note, one of the guys took a job to Exeter in Devon recently. Hours later he phoned the taxi desk in Terminal Three and said he thought he must have got lost, because he was in Cardiff: 'You ain't only got lost, sunshine,' replied the desk man, 'you're even in the wrong "effing" country!'

Another hilarious story concerns one of the guys returning from a nice long job in the country. He's heading down this country lane and comes to a level crossing with the barrier down and a train on its way. There's a couple of old geezers waiting to cross and one of them has got a scruffy old dog on a lead. Anyway, up comes the 'country squire' on his lovely white horse, and he waits till the barriers come up. Meanwhile, the old dog takes a dislike to the horse and barks fiercely at him. The country squire is nearly thrown off when the horse shies, so he gives the dog a whack with his riding crop. Now all hell breaks loose. The old boy ties the dog lead to the barrier and goes over to give the country squire a piece of his mind, and while the two of them are effing and blinding, suddenly, whoosh, and the train rushes by, closely followed by a dog yelping in pain. The barrier had gone up and the poor old dog had gone up with it, yelping like, well, like a mad dog being slowly strangled, I suppose!

My own particular funny story happened when I picked up this foreign guy and, in broken English, he asked to go to Mornington Crescent. That's great, I thought. Drop him off in Camden Town and straight home to Hampstead. Now comes the rub, I'm bombing it down the M4 and suddenly he's bashing on the window, so I pulled over on to the hard shoulder.

'What's up, guv?' I asked in a friendly manner. 'I was told,' he replied, 'that this address is very near to the airport.' So I asked him for the letter with the address on it and, lo and behold, it was Mornington Crescent, *Cranford*, literally outside the airport on the Bath Road! Luckily, he wasn't a bad guy and we came to some sort of compromise on the final fare. The most expensive mistake I ever made in my younger days was when I confused Bagshot, Berkshire, with Didcot, Oxfordshire, a difference of some 50 miles. I had priced the fare to Bagshot and when I eventually reached Didcot, it was over three times as much on the meter. It was my mistake, but the American family were quite sweet and very considerate and gave me a bit extra to compensate for my error.

On another occasion I was first cab on T1 and up walked a very nice Chinese gentleman who wanted to go to Brighton. This was a prime fare and all the other cabbies standing around talking were green with envy. I came to an agreed price with the gentleman, so imagine my surprise and dismay when we walked back to my cab and he suddenly said, quite definitely, 'No go in that taxi. Me only go in black taxi.'

Okay, so my cab was dark green, or to be perfectly precise, it was classified as British Racing Green. The trouble is that using a euphemism like 'Black Cab' invites foreigners to interpret it literally. This guy had quite rightly been warned beforehand about the risk of using un-licensed minicabs. But he wrongly assumed that all 'Black Cabs' were black! I showed him my Hackney Carriage plate, my taximeter and my Taxi licence. But all to no avail, he was adamant, he wanted a black 'Black Cab'.

By this time, all the cabbies behind me were curled up as I desperately tried to save a lucrative fare, especially the guy directly behind me who was rubbing his hands in eager anticipation. But he was also in for a shock. The Chinese guy refused to get into his dark blue cab, or the red cab that was third on the rank, or even the white cab at number four. So all four of us were left with egg on our faces!

I don't often lose my cool with passengers. The odd time I do, I count to ten and tell myself they will be getting out soon and not to get involved. But recently I had the misfortune to pick up this obnoxious little man on Terminal One. No please, no thank you, no kiss my a——, just a curt and very rude request, 'Wandsworth, cabbie, I'll tell you the road soon.' Okay, count to ten, don't bite and don't let him wind you up. Ten minutes or so elapsed while he looked up the street name in his briefcase. Then another rude request in the same tone, 'Maudling Road I want, do you know it?'

Did I know Maudling Road indeed? I hadn't been in Wandsworth since the eighties and it could have been High Street China for all I knew! 'No, I don't know it, sir,' I replied politely, 'but I'll stop the meter and look it up in the A–Z when we get nearer.' Then he starts mumbling on about London cabbies supposedly having a superior knowledge and why didn't I know Maudling Road? Still counting to ten, mind you I was near the hundred by now, I pulled into the kerb and got my map out and noticed my knuckles were getting white as I clenched the map. 'One hundred and one, one hundred and two, one hundred and three. . . .' Try as I might, I just couldn't find the name of the bloody road on my map. Out of the hundreds and hundreds of roads, I couldn't find the one this pillock wanted!

'I'm sorry, sir,' I said apologetically, 'I don't seem able to find it. I've tried all the Ms and all the M-As and all the M-A-Us, but I simply can't find it.' 'What are you talking about, you blithering idiot?' he shouted out. 'You spell it M-A-G-D-A-L-E-N, just like the Oxford College, but everyone knows it's pronounced Maudling.'

By this time I've counted up to around three hundred and there's steam coming out of my ears. I'd been polite and helpful, but I know when I've been 'stitched-up', as they say in the trade. 'Okay, smart arse,' I said getting out of my cab and sticking my ugly face and broken nose into his window, 'if you're such a clever dick and I'm only an ignorant peasant, why didn't the former Chancellor of the Exchequer Reginald Maudling spell his "effing" name M-A-G-D-A-L-E-N?'

Funny that, he didn't answer my question and he didn't say another word until he got to Magdalen Road. Then, lo and behold, he actually said 'please' when asking for a receipt. Suffice to say he didn't get his receipt, but he did get a piece of my tongue about being a pompous and obnoxious little man!

But every so often as a Heathrow cabbie, you are given the opportunity to do a good PR job for the trade. Take recently, when I was approached by a pleasant young American couple studying a map and the guy said to me, 'Hiya, cabbie, we wanna go to a little village near Cambridge, but we can't find it on the map.' 'No problem,' says I, not wanting to lose a good ride into the country. 'Jump in and we'll find it.'

So we came to some mutual agreement about the price and off we went heading for the M25. I looked in the mirror and saw they were still studying the map and shaking their heads. So I switched on the intercom and asked in a friendly voice, 'What's the name of the little village, sir?' Back came the answer that sounded like music to my ears and was almost certain to make me look impressive. This was almost too good to be true.

'I think you pronounce it Bassingbourne,' he replied. 'Oh yes,' I said knowingly, 'that's on the border of Hertfordshire and Cambridgeshire. Just find Royston on your map, then head north-east towards Cambridge and you'll find it.'

A couple of minutes later I heard a cry of delight from the back and the guy said with his voice filled with admiration, 'I've heard you London cabbies have got a super knowledge, but this is something else!' I took the praise in a diplomatic manner, just nodding sagely and telling him that London cabbies were the most highly-trained taxi-drivers anywhere in the world. We knew everything from London to Cambridge – and even farther afield. I then proceeded to tell him of my extensive knowledge of Stratford-on-Avon and Windsor Castle, just in case I could book them for a tour in the future. But I didn't have the heart to break the illusion and confess that I had spent most of my National Service at RAF Bassingbourne in the late fifties!

Heathrow Airport is such a vast, busy area that consequently it attracts low-life like the bag-snatchers, the pickpockets and the conmen operating the scams.

One of the chaps picked up these two guys and a foreign-looking lady recently on Terminal Three. They wanted to negotiate a price to Birmingham, stopping first at West Acton to pick something up. So the deal was done and off went the cab to West Acton. One of the guys jumped out and said he wouldn't be a minute, while the other guy kept looking at his watch and muttering, 'Where the bloody hell has he gone?'

At length, the second guy jumped out and said he'd sort out his mate and be back in a jiffy. Now the cabbie wasn't at all worried, he had the lady in the back and he wasn't at all suspicious at the turn of events. But, after a very long dwell, he did begin to get a little suspicious and turning around to the lady in the back he said politely, 'Have you got any idea where the gentlemen have gone, madam?' To his absolute horror, the lady replied in very broken English, 'I do not know them. I met them in the terminal and paid them £100 for my part of the taxi fare to Birmingham.'

Now the driver knows he's been conned. He calls the Ol' Bill and they discover she's an illegal immigrant with no valid papers and no more dough. So, the cabbie's done three hours in cold blood on the job, including his wait in the Taxi Feeder Park and the ride to West Acton, and he hasn't earned a brass farthing! And did he get any sympathy from his fellow cabbies when he told the story in the canteen? Did he hell!

Finally, the cabbie who got a nice hundred-pound ride into the wilds of the country. He copped his money, had a cup of tea and a sandwich, then put twenty pounds of diesel into his tank – or so he thought. His cab suddenly started to backfire and stutter on his way back and the driver realised he'd filled it up with petrol and not diesel. He managed to limp to the next garage and they drained his tank at the cost of eighty quid! So, he had absolutely no dough left from the fare and had to use his credit card for some more diesel to get him home! It's so horrendous, it's funny, innit?

COMETH THE MOMENT, COMETH THE MAN

What makes a hero is one of those imponderables. Are we born brave, or do we suddenly become blindly brave in a desperate and life-threatening situation?

Take the case of London cabbie Michael O'Leary. Now Mike, who works at Heathrow regularly, would be the first to admit that he is a most unlikely hero. He's 66 years old, father of six kids, with probably a gaggle of grandkids, and so terribly quiet and polite, you wouldn't think he'd say boo to a goose. So why would a mature grandfather, a bit wobbly on his pins, risk life and limb by sprinting (well, jogging anyway) across to the middle lane of the perilous M4 motorway, to save the life of a motorist who had collapsed in his car with a severe heart attack?

This is a true account of a very brave London cabbie. It's March 2000, around 4 p.m. and Mike is poodling empty out to Heathrow in the inside lane, doing a steady 45 mph. He notices a four-door saloon car moving slowly on the hard shoulder. The car has got its left indicator flashing, but is edging out into the middle lane. So Mike pulls past the car on the hard shoulder and from his high vantage point in his cab, he sees that the driver has collapsed with his head leaning back on the seat. By this time the car has reached the middle lane of the motorway and is moving slowly and erratically into the very busy fast lane.

So Mike parks his cab and dashes across to the middle lane in the hope of stopping the car, which is now moving at around 10 mph. Despite the screeching of horns and motorists yelling out that he must be 'effing mad', Mike manages to open the passenger door and, holding on to the central partition with the other hand, jumps into the car and falls in a heap on the floor. He manages to steer the car back to the hard shoulder, then knocks it out of gear and applies the handbrake.

Mike thought the motorist was dead. Luckily, while

he was phoning for an ambulance, another motorist with a knowledge of first aid stopped to try and resuscitate the guy. Even more luck was to follow a couple of minutes later. A passing ambulance noticed the incident and the paramedics took over. Thanks to Mike's bravery and the help he received afterwards, the guy survived a major heart attack.

In his phone call to me, Mike said, 'My days of fast footwork are long gone, but for a few vital seconds, I managed to turn the clock back.' I knew his story was being told on the BBC's 999 show and I remarked somewhat cynically that he must have earned a nice few quid from four days filming. 'Yes and no, Alf,' he replied. 'I don't want people to know this, but I gave the fee to the guy who had the heart attack.'

Not only brave, but generous and caring as well.

THE HEATHROW EXPRESS (THE HEX)

Back in the early nineties, we were hearing on the grapevine that the BAA were planning to build a state-of-the-art railway link from Paddington Station direct to Heathrow Airport. According to my information, their ultimate plan was to make Heathrow the very epicentre of a rail network, with links from Waterloo, St Pancras and eventually a rail link with the Thames Valley Trains and even the Great West Trains from Cornwall.

The main rail link from Paddington to just north of

Heathrow was already in place. What they had got to do after the contracts were signed and stations were built in the Central area was to tunnel under the Spur Road from the M4, a distance of some three miles, and link up with the existing lines. Despite the well-documented tunnel collapse at Terminal Three and a hold-up in the construction, about £440 million later, the project was complete and the cab trade's largest and most expensive competitor was up and running with a blaze of publicity.

The HEX was a formidable opponent. It had been built with private money and the BAA had managed to persuade the then Conservative Government that it shouldn't come under the rules of the Rail Regulator. That meant it could hike its fares up at any time, or make special deals. In effect, it could basically do what it liked! Many of the wise old heads in the trade realised at once the threat to our present client base at Heathrow. I myself reckoned the HEX would initially take at least twenty per cent of taxi passengers from day one and maybe an even bigger percentage as the word got around. The sad thing is that the trade had known about the HEX for years before it was constructed and we had a God-sent opportunity to get our act together by formulating a competitive pricing structure and setting up a local rank system. Way back before the HEX was even constructed, we had a meeting with the then BAA Managing Director, Mike Roberts, and he more or less told us the future of licensed taxis at Heathrow. I quote what he said verbatim: 'I foresee the future of licensed taxis at Heathrow as being in the periphery of the airport.'

But again internal politics reared its ugly head and the warring factions couldn't agree on what most people at the time perceived as a perfectly good local rank system to secure our future at Heathrow.

The BAA's next obvious step in order to expand their massive investment was to market the HEX worldwide. This soon happened when they started selling Heathrow Express tickets through their travel shops in the UK. Next came travel shops all over Europe and in the States, with HEX tickets linked with package holidays and free trips to a stately home and, later, to the BAA's London Eye. The BAA got it right most of the way but in my opinion, they made a big mistake by hiking up the single fare, from an already expensive £10 for a single second-class journey, to £12. They also made a mistake by advertising Paddington as being in 'the middle of Central London'. It didn't take too long for the airline regulars to do their sums and realise that at twelve quid a time, plus a taxi at the other end to their final destination, it added up to well over the price of a shared taxi into town. So many of our regulars returned, but still the cab trade at Heathrow dithered with apathy and still they couldn't agree on a united policy. In fact, it became almost farcical when the original opponents of the local rank system came back some three years later and presented an almost identical system. But that's the cab trade in a nutshell. We've had almost a virtual monopoly at Heathrow for over fifty years and that monopoly is now deeply rooted with apathy. Some drivers honestly believe that it's their God-given right to have the stage to themselves at Heathrow. But the world doesn't stand still, and they could be in for a mighty big shock in the near future!

CONCORDE

Most of this piece was written just a few short months before the terrible Concorde crash in Paris. Nevertheless, I still believe Concorde is a wonderful plane and am glad to see it flying again. Even after three decades of supersonic flight, there's still no finer sight to see at Heathrow than Concorde roaring down the runway at 250 mph. I watch in fascination from the Taxi Feeder Park as this mighty bird takes to the sky on its daily flight to New York. The sound is as mighty as the sight!

Concorde passengers tell me that the lethal acceleration of the aircraft literally pins you to your seat and in under half an hour the plane is ten and a half miles above the earth's surface, on the very edge of outer space and travelling at twice the speed of sound. Just three hours and seventeen minutes later, Concorde will land at New York's JFK Airport. Because passengers spend only half as much time in the air compared to conventional planes, and because Concorde's cabin pressure is much higher, people rarely suffer the queasy symptoms of jet-lag. No wonder then that the 'high-flyers' of the business world are more than happy to cough up in excess of £5,500 for a return ticket. That works out at almost a thousand pounds per hour!

But amazingly, and with some sadness, it would appear that the end is in sight, not only for Concorde, but for the whole dream of supersonic passenger transport. In less than a decade, the twelve Concordes in service will be retired and the first age of supersonic transport will have come to an end. Which begs the pertinent question, why scrap the finest and most advanced flying machine the world has ever seen? As usual it's all down to profit and loss. Way back in the sixties when Concorde was first conceived, the airline experts were predicting that by the mid-seventies SSTs (supersonic transports) would become the standard aircraft of the ordinary passenger. But these experts couldn't foresee rising oil prices and economic woes across the world. And they couldn't foresee the coming of the lumbering 747 Jumbo Jet and the vast amount of revenue this aircraft could generate. So today most aviation development programmes are aimed at the super-jumbo, capable of carrying a massive five or six hundred passengers. I'm no expert, but surely scrapping a supersonic programme and then introducing massive, lumbering super-jumbos is a retrograde step for the aviation industry and is purely motivated by profit.

But various events have conspired to seal the fate of these marvellous aircraft. I wonder if future generations will look back and mock a decision to abandon progress for the benefits of profitability?

THE FUTURE OF TAXIS AT HEATHROW

I've always been a people-watcher and I find their different attitudes to life quite fascinating. And watching my fellow cabbies for many years – especially the Heathrow cabbies – I've come to the sad conclusion that many of them are cursed with an inherent trait for self-destruction. This tends to manifest itself in the form of apathy, greed, jealousy and even downright bloody-mindedness at times.

Take the apathy for starters. Whether this stems from being licensed by Parliament for over three hundred years, I'm not sure. But nothing is forever, even a world-famous taxi trade that is second to none. The youngsters coming into the trade are convinced they can always get a living on their cab, even though in the future they could well be doing many hours a day to achieve that. Then the more mature drivers have this apathetic saying about 'only having four or five years to go until retirement', so 'they ain't bothered about the future of the trade'.

As for the greed, that comes with some drivers grossly over-pricing fares outside the Metropolitan Police District (MPD), knowing full well that these punters will never take a London taxi to that destination ever again. Multiply that many hundreds of times every week and you've got the reason for the almost total disappearance of any 'Windsors' and 'Sloughs' and the like. The jealousy and bloody-mindedness arises when some conscientious and caring cabmen try to set up organisations for the betterment of the trade. These people are never judged on their results and hard work. Oh no, it's wrongly assumed that they are lining their own pockets and the bloody-minded drivers refuse to join and become a united force to be reckoned with.

But the licensed trade should be extremely bothered with the advent of minicab licensing, or Private Hire Vehicles (PHVs) as they are now known, and I believe the biggest threat will be directed at Heathrow. The shrewd businessmen running these large, traded PHV companies will have already done their homework about the vast potential of profits at Heathrow. They will have obtained the exact throughput of cabs every day of the week and every week of the year – by fair means or foul. They will convert all of these taxi journeys into an average fare and come up with more or less the final total. And that final total will have them rushing in for part of the action, because you're talking millions of pounds every year with any future operation.

In defence of the Heathrow regulars, they have proved in the past that they are far more unified than the 'town drivers'. A decade or so ago, they all voted to form their own cooperative and to raise money on the gate for a Taxi Desk in Terminal One. As the cooperative grew and became more businesslike, so fully-manned Taxi Desks were installed in T2, T3 and T4. These desks were manned by experienced ex-taxi drivers who had lost their licences through ill-health. It was a great PR job for our trade and did a lot to convince the BAA that cabbies could actually organise a business venture successfully. Every time the drivers buy a credit, a small sum is added on to pay the wages of the desk men. This was a great concept in funding our own trade and should have put us way out of reach of any future opposition. Heathrow Airport Licensed Taxis, or HALT, the name of their cooperative, had a seven or eight-year start before the opposition appeared. By virtue of sheer hard graft they got the four Taxi Desks into place, started a popular fixed-price voucher scheme and credit card facility. In fact, with the full support of all the regulars, the 'ship' would now be well in place to repel any 'boarders'. But unfortunately, in real life it doesn't happen like that. Owing to a mixture of personalities, the lack of a quorum at AGMs, internal politics and, yes, jealousy, HALT has been isolated and a decade of hard work has been lost. Again, in all fairness, I must admit to having being a founder member of HALT and its chairman and editor of the HALT magazine for around six years. So, the outcome is particularly painful for me.

The door is now wide open for the PHVs to get their foot in. The BAA are already advertising for large fleets of limos suitable for a pre-booking service. The idea was already touted to the drivers by HALT, who fully understood that a major pre-booking service was vital. But the apathy and the jealousies and the bloody-mindedness reared their ugly heads once more and they turned it down flat. And why? Simply because it was organised by HALT! What you need to remember is that the BAA doesn't get any revenue from the cabbies, even though by law they have to have them on the airport. But franchises with the major PHV companies could mean big business for them. And if, in the future, when they eventually expand their pre-booking operation and can succeed in cutting off the cabbie's client base at source, that is, the Taxi Ranks on all four terminals, then, in theory, the cabbies won't be getting many fares and won't bother to rank up at Heathrow any more. Consequently, if this future scenario does occur, the cabbies won't require two large feeder parks, will they? So the pre-booked PHVs will possibly have the use of one feeder park as a holding area and buy their way in with booking desks in all four, or possibly five terminals. They will display menu boards, just like at Gatwick, quoting reasonable set prices all over the country and quite possibly corner the market. Then, and only then, will the Heathrow cabbie finally realise that the world moves on, and that by their own intransigence over the past years they have got left behind.

Take Terminal Five as a classic example. T5 Inquiry Inspector Roy Vandermeer QC handed his report of recommendations from the Public Inquiry to the Government just before Christmas 2000. It's odds-on that T5 will go ahead, but what are we doing about it to secure our ranks in the new terminal? Zilch! I sincerely hope my predictions are way out, but only time will tell.

SEVEN

FAREWELL TO NIGHT WORK

Things had to change, and not only for the benefit of my family. The street culture of New York had reached London by the eighties and working nights on the cab was proving to be perilous. I could handle drunks and loud-mouthed yobs and I could handle the odd punter spewing all over the back of my cab. But the stories I was hearing in the shelters from cabmen who had been bilked, threatened with knives and guns – and even with a syringe that supposedly contained the Aids virus – convinced me that the time was ripe for a change.

I had heard horrendous tales of cabmen being directed into South London housing estates, then the barred gate would be closed by another of the gang and they couldn't get out unscathed until the moneybag was handed over. One of the guys, Italian Dino, was so petrified when it happened to him, that he rammed the barred gate the gang were sitting on and smashed the front of his cab beyond repair. Then the press started calling London cabbies racists, because none of the cabs would accept a black guy going South. That's rubbish. Take it from someone who believes that there is good and bad in all races, but I have seen the figures on cab muggings that the police decided not to publish, for fear of attracting copycat muggers. It certainly wasn't racism, it's called self-preservation. And if the figures proved that it was mainly Chinese who were doing the mugging at that time, then London cabbies would have steered well clear of Chinese!

The final incident that convinced me I had to change my lifestyle happened in Willesden one St Patrick's Night. I was cruising slowly down the High Road looking for a fare to take me near home and saw this attractive young lady flag me down. She had a guy with her and they were having a cuddle, so I thought, they'll be no problem, and I stopped. She opened the door and got in the back with him and suddenly yelled, 'Drag him out here quickly, Pat.'

I had been well and truly set up, with her as the decoy. Two massive guys came out of the shop doorway literally dragging another guy, threw him into my cab and jumped in themselves. Now I knew I was in trouble. 'Will you drop three of us off in Kilburn?' said the girl. 'And the other two will be going on to Victoria Station.'

I weighed up my options calmly. I might stand a chance once I got shot of the three in Kilburn. After all, I thought, there will be plenty of people around in Victoria. It worked out smoothly, they dragged the guy out in Kilburn and I continued on to Victoria, but that's when the trouble started. I pulled up alongside the taxi rank in Wilton Road and told them the fare. 'Bejasus,' said the one built like a brick wall, 'we'll not be paying that much.' Here we go again, I thought. So I got out to try and reason with them. The other guy, who was paralytic drunk, threw a punch at me and I just pushed him on to the floor. Then up came the one built like a brick wall. He grabbed my brand-new, green-striped shirt with one massive hand, but because he was drunk, he'd grabbed it with his right hand and now he couldn't throw a punch. So, to protect myself, I started hammering him with right and left hooks to the stomach. Suddenly, his legs went, and he slid down onto his knees ripping every button off my brand-new shirt. Some of the cabbies came off the rank and told me the Ol' Bill had been called, so we dragged the two guys into the kerb and the cabbies made a space for me on the rank. Minutes later the police wagon arrived and they chucked them inside. Naturally, when I arrived home looking in a terrible state, my wife said, 'That's the finish of it, you're going on day work!'

CABBING INTO THE TWENTY-FIRST CENTURY

There's a saying in the cab trade that's been adapted from the Army: 'Old cabmen never die, they only fade away.' This saying is particularly significant in our business because cabbies, just as long as they pass their annual medical after they reach the age of 65, can continue with their profession on a part-time basis, or even for one day a week. Some cab garages find it very profitable to reserve a couple of 'old boys' cabs. One cab alone may be shared by four or five part-timers, all doing just one day a week. Consequently, the fleet owner will get a bigger return than if he rented out the cab on the weekly flat-rate.

You would have read the quote from the Taxi and Omnibus White Paper of 1895 in an earlier chapter. This stated that the lifestyle of the Victorian cabbies wasn't 'inclined to longevity'. Not so today. I believe there are cabmen in their late eighties and early nineties, still holding a licence and still doing a little bit of cabbing to help supplement their pensions. But, and this is a worry, many more cabmen, some only in their thirties and forties, are suffering from heart attacks and having their licences revoked for three years or more, or maybe permanently. Many more of these basically young guys are keeling over with fatal heart attacks and leaving behind young families. It's all to do with pressure. Pressure to pay for the big mortgage every month for twenty-five years. Pressure to pay for the new cab and pressure to feed and clothe their families. I've learned from years of experience. Go out to work nice and relaxed, do a few hours, then stop for a cuppa. Then work for another few more hours and when finally that lovely passenger comes up to you and asks for an address near your home, call it a day.

But when these guys under pressure leave home early in the morning to miss the rush hour, they have a sum of money stored in their heads that they *must* make in one day to pay all the bills. We've all been there and we've all been under that pressure in the past. But cabbing in London is the hardest job in the world if, before you start, you set yourself a target. It may well be a very quiet day on the streets, maybe long queues of cabs at every station and at Heathrow. That's when the pressure begins and, come lunchtime, when you're only holding a fraction of what you set out to take, you're ready to blow in sheer frustration.

I learned my lesson many years ago when some of my best mates in the trade started keeling over. It was the same story being told at every funeral. 'Poor old Mick (or Joe, or Terry) – he was a right grafter.' Indeed, he was – they were! But what's the point of having a posh house, a boat on the river and a timeshare flat in Tenerife, if it kills you in the process? We are all going to keel over at one time or another, but in my case, it certainly won't be from overwork!

My advice to the youngsters coming into the trade is try and not overstretch yourself by budgeting from your first few months on the road. Every Butterboy sits on the cab for long hours when they first get out and those takings are not the norm. Believe me, you'll soon get browned off with the long hours and settle in to a regular weekly routine. Most importantly, join one of the trade organisations. You may well require their legal experts in the future and you'll certainly need the cover of their sick schemes to help feed your family if you happen to have a bad illness or accident.

It might cost you a few quid every month, but at least it will enable you to sleep soundly at night!

Cabbing in London has changed dramatically over forty years. For a start, there are now around twice as many cabs and drivers on the road and just about everybody uses cabs every day. Strangely enough, this change of public perception towards using cabs is mainly thanks to our opposition, the minicabs. In the old days the ordinary working-class used cabs only for weddings, funerals and holidays. And, late at night after the theatres burst, the only unaccompanied women hailing taxis would almost certainly be one of the girls on the game. But the advent and popular usage of minicabs at all times by the younger age groups has without doubt contributed significantly to the increase in the usage of the London taxi. No longer are we a rich person's mode of transport. No longer do we have to rank up outside the many gentlemen's clubs in St James at lunchtimes, waiting for 'Their Lordships' to come out three-parts boozed then take them to the House of Lords, where they will have a kip all the afternoon and be able to draw their daily 'appearance' money.

In the old days, any City gent or businessman was known among cabbies as a 'toff', or a 'bowler hat'. I well remember my late brother-in-law telling me about the time in the late fifties when he was crossing over Charing Cross Road from Leicester Square, with a bowler hat in the back. Suddenly, he had to brake like a madman to avoid a police car that had shot the red lights. The police car pulled up with a screech of brakes and out jumped two flash young coppers. They started giving my brother-in-law some verbal about not giving way to a police car on an emergency call and accusing him of careless driving. Their attitude changed dramatically when the rear door of the cab opened and out stepped the bowler hat. In fact, they looked as though they were going to be violently sick as they saluted smartly. The bowler hat turned out to be none other than the then Commissioner of the Metropolitan Police, Sir John Nott-Bower. He walked angrily up to the two flash coppers and demanded, 'Why wasn't your bell ringing if you were on a call?'

The two coppers started to turn a bright red and both mumbled something inaudible. But Sir John wasn't finished yet and he demanded their numbers and what station they were from. Finally, said my brother-in-law, Sir John said to the sheepish pair, 'If you are happy to apologise to the cabbie for your rudeness, maybe he won't take his complaint any farther with me as a witness.'

It's a cracking little story of someone in authority having to eat humble pie, isn't it?

Another bowler hat story involves myself this time. I was heading down The Strand a while back and was suddenly confronted by this young copper who waved me down. He strolled cockily around to my side of the cab and said, 'I'm nicking you, cabbie, for jumping the traffic lights.' I protested my innocence and said I didn't have a clue to what he was talking about. Anyway, the bowler hat jumps out, asks the copper for his number and says in a loud voice to me, 'If there is any problem, cabbie, come and see me in my chambers, here's my card.'

Now the young copper is not so cocky. He doesn't want to get involved with lawyers or solicitors, or maybe even a barrister. So he just mumbles something about 'Watch it next time', and beats a hasty retreat. The bowler hat paid me off at Charing Cross Station, including a nice fat tip and when I went to thank him for his help, he just grinned and walked away. Later, when I looked at his card I saw the reason for his grin: it read 'Bert Smith, Fruit and Vegetable Merchant. Piazza Chambers, Covent Garden'.

I really enjoy the interesting cross-section of society using cabs in this era and, by and large, they are really very pleasant to talk to on many differing topics. And it does help if you have a smile on your face and say 'Good morning' to them!

CABBIE BY DAYLIGHT

Around seventeen years ago, when the first of my children decided to get married, soon followed by the other two, who wanted to share a flat with friends, I decided the time was right to try my very hardest to work in the day. Working at night wasn't fair on my wife. We'd started off together as friends and lovers and I wanted us to be friends and lovers in our maturing years. During my years of night work, I had seen many marriages break up because the cabbie had been involved with one of the club girls, or the lonely wife had met a new man at one of her bingo nights. To be perfectly honest, there was another reason for packing up working at night, apart from the punch-ups with drunks, and it was a scary one. Our lovely, fully-grown Doberman bitch just loved sleeping on our bed. The trouble with Dobermans is they get very possessive and there came a point when she would growl at me as I tried to get into the bed. As if that wasn't bad enough, a few nights later she stood menacingly at the bedroom door, the hairs upright on the back of her neck and her teeth bared in a wicked snarl and just wouldn't let me in! The first reason for my reverting back to day work is the truth, but my temperamental Doberman convinced me I needed to face the rigours of the London traffic – for my own safety!

Other mature cabbies will tell you it's very difficult to change your habits of two decades. And so it was with me. My body clock had been set to go to bed late and get up late. I tried very hard but I just couldn't get used to getting up early. So, my first two efforts at working days slowly turned into afternoons and early evenings. The transition was very slow and very traumatic, especially the frightening London traffic. Again, after all the years of driving a cab at night, I was on another learning curve. Once again I needed to re-learn the art of working in the day. Even the positions of the station taxi ranks had changed, especially Paddington. Instead of getting on to the rank by turning in from Bishops Bridge Road and going into the heart of the station, now, with the advent of the Heathrow Express, the taxi rank stretched the whole length down the centre of Eastbourne Terrace. But I stuck at it and eventually I succeeded in changing a lifestyle of two decades.

But over those years London and its population had also changed dramatically. The increased violence and road-rage was all rather scary. No longer was it the norm to have just an argument with another driver. I've seen smartly-dressed guys jump out of their cars in a blind rage and start kicking the doors of another car. A friend of mine who runs a cabbies' café was driving home a few years back. He stopped at a zebra crossing to allow people to cross and started to pull away when it looked clear. Suddenly an angry face appeared alongside, accusing him of not stopping. My friend said he hadn't seen the guy and the fella seemed to slap him on the face and walked off in a huff. As my mate carried on driving, he felt a coldness in his face and looked into the driving mirror to see that it was pouring with blood. The guy hadn't slapped his face, he had sliced it from top to bottom with a razor-sharp Stanley knife! Now my mate looks more like Al Capone than a café owner.

It's quite common nowadays to see drivers scrapping outside their cars over some soppy incident and, unfortunately, there never seem to be any police officers on the beat to sort things out anymore. As for me, my fighting days are over. Any kind of aggro, and my windows go up, my central locking goes on and I just sit and smile while the geezer goes purple in the face. I've found from many years of experience, it takes two to make an argument and if the other guy won't play his part, then it becomes really frustrating just swearing at yourself! I tell a lie, I did get out of my cab recently after I had done a diabolical U-turn outside Harrods in heavy traffic. The guy who I had cut up gave me a blast on his horn as he went past and as the lights at the Scotch House were on red, I got out of my cab and approached the driver. He'd seen me coming in his mirror and it couldn't have been a pretty sight. Six feet tall, big and burly and with a nose that looked as though it had been used as a punch bag by Mike Tyson. 'I'm terribly sorry about that incident,' I said, as the driver looked at me warily. 'It was completely my fault,' I continued, 'and I apologise unreservedly.'

Now the guy is totally confused and bemused. He was expecting fisticuffs or verbal abuse at the worst. Instead of that, he's got this big ugly geezer eating humble pie and apologising. He stared long and hard at me for a couple of seconds, probably just satisfying himself that it wasn't a con. 'Well, er, er,' he spluttered, 'try thinking about other drivers before you pull those strokes again.' 'Okay mate, thanks for that,' I said, 'have a good day.'

And that was that. No fisticuffs, no expletives and no high blood pressure. He was happy because he'd won the moral fight and had a good tale to tell his friends about this cabbie the size of a brick wall, who had been ground into an abject apology. And I was happy because I had proven that a genuine apology takes away any violence in a confrontational situation. How can you possibly want to fight someone who is obviously eating humble pie?

After about six months I finally got in the swing of working days and I was quite enjoying it, especially coming home at night and sitting down with a drink to watch telly. It was very civilised. I assumed – quite wrongly as it turned out – that working in the day would get rid of the aggro, the runners and bilkers. Not a bit of it. Up he came after I had eventually worked my way to the point of Fenchurch Street taxi rank. He was in his forties, dressed a bit scruffily, wearing trainers and carrying a large black plastic rubbish bag, half-full of whatever. 'I want the corner of Southwark Park Road and Jamaica Road as the first stop, mate,' he said, 'and then on to Surrey Quays, is that all right?' 'No problem, guv,' I said, suppressing a groan at the thought of the evening traffic chaos across Tower Bridge. I'll give him his due, he certainly knew the back doubles after seeing the traffic tailback at Dockhead and, before I knew it, we were in Southwark Park Road facing Jamaica Road. 'I'll leave the gear in the back, mate, and I'll be back in a jiffy,' he said, crossing the road to an archway leading to a block of flats. Up to that very moment I hadn't even considered anything dodgy. He had been pleasant and chatty and said he did the same journey twice a week. But, just as he was about to enter the arch, he looked back over his shoulder and grinned at me. I knew then that he had bilked me.

As a nightman for many years, I really should have tumbled the 'old bag' con, it's as old as the hills. Leave a bag full of whatever in the back and it's human nature that the driver will assume the punter is coming back to pick it up. What can I say to defend myself? Maybe I'm getting too trusting after all those years on the cab. Yes, the bag on the back seat was full of tin cans and bottles and, yes, I had been well and truly legged over for about seven quid. Now if I'm in the City late afternoons, I tend to put on at Fenchurch Street in the hope of meeting my friend from Southwark Park Road. I'm saving something special for him out of his big black bag – and it ain't a tin can!

Every so often something happens while you're driving a cab in London that stays forever in your mind. The following story never fails to 'fill me with emulsion'! It was just another common or garden Saturday morning, or so I thought. I found a fare straight away outside Hampstead Station down to Little Venice, then immediately picked up a young couple at the roundabout outside the big builders' merchants. Because he was carrying this huge five-litre tin of paint, I remember wondering at the time what colour they were going to paint their flat. Little did I realise I was going to discover their colour scheme much sooner than I had ever anticipated! 'Could we go first to the bank opposite Little Venice in Edgware Road?' he said. 'No problem, sir,' said I, nice and relaxed and chirpy. Next: 'Could you turn left into Sutherland Avenue and stop at the far end?' says he. 'No problem, sir,' said I, still nice and relaxed and chirpy.

No problem, that is, until I did a sharp left turn and heard the ominous clonk of a heavy tin object hitting the rubber mat in the back of the cab. My fears were realised when frantic shouts of 'Stop the cab, stop the cab' came from behind me and I got out to see that they were going to use a very attractive cream emulsion for their flat. The trouble was most of the five litres were seeping out of my offside door! My red cab looked like an ice-cream van with a dodgy fridge and all the ice cream melted. My first reaction was to blow my top but, what the hell, I thought, what is done is done. I opened the offside door with some trepidation and the sight I saw was so bizarre I couldn't help but chuckle. Have you ever seen two people in the back of a taxi paddling about in two inches of cream emulsion? The young woman was in a state of shock and all she kept shouting was, 'I really think we should sue the paint company for not screwing on the lid tight enough, don't you, James, don't you, James, don't you, James?'

As for James, well at least he got it together – mind you, the paint was considerably deeper on his side! He leapt out of the nearside door, put the almost empty can of paint under the step, then proceeded to scrape it back into the tin with a large piece of cardboard, saying hopefully, 'We might save a fraction, darling, if we're lucky.'

After a temporary mopping-up job with old pieces of rags and lots and lots of tissues, it was decided to go to their house and complete the job with a mop and buckets of water. While they were busy beavering away in the back, I got through on the radio to ask if anyone had any ideas to help with the cleaning up. I wish I hadn't bothered, what a load of corny old plonkers! The despatcher started the ball rolling by saying gleefully that everyone was filled with 'emulsion' by my plight. Then another bright spark put in his two pennyworth by saying 'I shouldn't try and gloss over this situation' and that 'I can't brush it off lightly!'

Ask a silly question and you're bound to get a silly answer. I had done nearly two hours in cold blood by this time and they were still scrubbing away in the back. The young woman was doing her Gunga Din bit with numerous buckets of water, while the fella was literally covered from head to foot in cream emulsion. They kept repeating how terribly sorry they were and how could they make it up to me. My cunning brain immediately registered pound notes as compensation, but I relented and thought how could I possibly charge a very nice couple for a complete accident? I mean, cream emulsion paint is not quite the same as a drunk being 'Tom and Dick' in the back, is it? Anyway, as we say in cab trade parlance, I wiped my mouth and drove off, with the back of my cab as clean and shiny as it had been for many a year.

As God is my witness, I was sitting on the Warwick Avenue cab rank the following week and noticed a middle-aged Asian couple approaching me. The guy was carrying, would you believe it, a large five-litre tin of paint. I started the engine a bit lively and shot away like a bat out of hell! And that ain't racism, it's cream emulsion.

Some stories you hear from fellow drivers are often so serious that you can't help but laugh. Take this mate of mine they call 'St Albans' Phil. He's never at a loss for words and he's got what we Londoners call plenty of 'rabbit'. Anyway, a while back Phil was heading for home up the Barnet Way. The traffic was very bad due to the major road-works in progress and it was while he was passing one of the many working JCBs that the driver, without any warning, suddenly spun his digger around and those awesome steel teeth ripped open the whole nearside of the cab. Bang went the central pillar, down came the roof of the cab and as the teeth hooked in, Phil felt himself being lifted into the air in an almost dreamlike scenario. Poor old Phil, he had to be cut out of his cab, rushed to hospital in an ambulance where they plastered over his sore bits, but nothing serious.

So he'd had a bad day moneywise, his cab was a complete write-off and he even had to hail a cab to get him home from the hospital. After patiently listening to his tale of woe his good lady wife said, as lady wives tend to say, 'That's terrible, darling, but did you remember to bring in the evening paper?' The guys tell me that Phil was actually speechless for the very first time in his life!

Probably the most horrendous and frightening story I have ever heard was told to me by a cab acquaintance. His teenage son and his mates had booked a boozy weekend in Amsterdam. They had some drinks on the ferry, some drinks in their hotel after dinner and made their way to the red-light district to find a lively strip club. During the course of a boozy evening one of the lads was seen chatting up an attractive, busty blonde. When it was time to leave, there was no sign of their mate or the busty blonde. When they all got up the next morning there was still no sign of their mate, and the lads were all laughing and joking and saying what a lucky devil he was to have cracked it on the very first night. But, as afternoon approached, they started to get worried about him missing the ferry and decided to call the police. He was eventually found wandering about near the hotel in what the police wrongly assumed was a drunken stupor.

The lads took him back to the hotel room and tried to sober him up, but he kept groaning in agony and puking up all over his clothes. So they took off his shirt and were horrified to see a massive, freshly-stitched scar across his waist and around his back. The poor kid wasn't drunk at all. He had been set up by the busty blonde, and drugged and butchered by a back-street surgeon to illegally remove one of his kidneys.

There is a thriving black market on the continent for young, healthy kidneys for transplants and some of the poorest families actually consent to this operation to feed their kids. But this innocent young lad was deliberately lured to a place in a drugged state and cut open like some lump of meat – shocking.

I had worked at Heathrow during my spell on night work and, to give myself a break from the traffic, I started going out there empty around lunchtime. You certainly don't earn big bucks just sitting in the Taxi Feeder Park for hours on end. But it was an easy life and gave me the opportunity to write some copy. Then, around ten years ago, I was invited to get involved in formulating the cabbie's cooperative HALT, Heathrow Airport Licensed Taxis. The cooperative took off in a big way with the full support of all the regulars at Heathrow and before long most of my week was taken up with HALT business and not driving a cab, especially when we started the magazine and I was in sole charge. Suddenly, it was all about getting copy and advertising in on time and all about deadlines. The magazine grew from an original eight pages in black and white to twelve. Then, to sixteen pages in colour and, eventually, twenty pages. I barely had time to do very much cabbing, but I was in my element, I thoroughly enjoyed the pressures every month.

Unfortunately, over a period of years HALT became isolated from its members. This was due to a number of reasons, like not being able to attain a quorum at their AGMs, thus enabling new faces to get elected on to the Committee, and the old chestnut of personalities becoming authoritarian and insular. Looking back in hindsight this was a crying shame because the concept of HALT was, and still is, a great idea. The BAA collected the HALT money on the entry charge to pay the wages of the desk men, while the HALT Committee busied themselves generating contracts to bring in extra work for the drivers. Instead of that, after seven or eight fruitful years when an awful lot was achieved, we now have a sad scenario where just a handful are left on the HALT Committee, while the vast majority of the drivers don't want anything to do with the cooperative.

So, instead of having plans and contracts in place to

protect the trade's client base at Heathrow against the inevitable arrival of the newly-licensed PHVs (Private Hire Vehicles) we now have a situation where the cab trade is totally fragmented and it looks like everyone for themselves. As I stated previously in my Heathrow chapter, the future's not looking too rosy for the cab trade. I've found from long experience that the London Cab trade is like a sleeping giant and it doesn't seem to move until it's too late. My advice is, wake up to the real world, guys and gals!

THE FUTURE OF THE FAMOUS LONDON CABBIE

With the licensing of minicabs in London, now known as PHVs, the cab trade faces its biggest ever battle. At the time of writing this book, a massive 40,000 'minicabbies' were waiting to be licensed by the Public Carriage Office. Just for starters, that's almost double the number of cabbies on the road and I've no doubt there will be many more as the PHV companies get their acts together.

As I perceive the future, there are two scenarios. We can bury our heads in the sand, as many of us did when the minicabs first hit the streets of London in 1961, and forfeit most of the lucrative account work built up by the radio circuits over many years. Not forgetting the major hotel chains, possibly, signing up with the PHV companies for fixed-price journeys for their guests, thus ensuring that the once-busy cab ranks outside suddenly become a nice place to have an uninterrupted kip! Whether the PHVs will manage to infiltrate the main-line railway termini and attack our client base will, I believe, require a change in the law. But nothing is cast in stone, even though the union has just won a court judgment up North concerning the same subject. They have successfully proven that a railway station is a public place and that PHVs are not allowed to be seen empty in any public place. But will the same apply to London in the future, especially when the full weight of the cab trade demonstrating outside Victoria Coach Station for the removal of the minicab desk inside failed to win success? So, if a railway station was deemed to be a 'public place', why not a coach station? I'm not saying the Law is an ass, what I am saying is that we won't ever win our biggest battle just with the help of the Law.

So what to do if we don't bury our heads in the sand? Trade unity is the first consideration because, if we are not united, we might just as well throw in the towel right now. Again, because our trade is so fragmented, this could be a problem. Many years ago, I advocated that every Butterboy on receiving his badge should be told to join one of the trade organisations. But at the time the PCO wasn't interested and now with the change in the law it's illegal to have a closed shop. We have now reached the sorry state of affairs where less than a third of London cabbies belong to any trade organisation, and even those who do are squabbling among themselves.

Even though many people ridicule them as having vested interests, we do have the Taxi Board as an important link to Government and MPs. The Taxi Board will be vitally important in our future battle against the PHVs and, instead of ridiculing them, maybe we should be supporting them and working alongside.

It's always been my sincere belief that the famous custom-built cab is essential to our future and I also believe that without the PCO's stringent Conditions of Fitness, especially the 25-ft turning circle, we wouldn't have a custom-built cab today. But, much to my surprise, there's a groundswell of opinion in the trade that advocates a relaxing of these stringent Conditions of Fitness, allowing MPVs, Multi-Purpose Vehicles, to operate as London taxis. I fully understand that the various trade organisations have got to react to the wishes of their members, some of whom are vehemently opposed to the very expensive and slightly antiquated custom-built cab. But, without wanting to sound too melodramatic, I honestly believe our cab is the last remaining ace in our ever diminishing, 300-year-old hand. Like any other owner-driver, or 'musher' as we are called (again, don't ask me where that word originates from, it sounds more like somebody driving a sleigh!), I would dearly love to save around ten grand on buying an MPV. But by saving that money on an MPV, we could easily lose 300 years of our history. Designer gear doesn't come cheap because it costs extra to be unique. Our custom-built cab is a designer vehicle and that's why we are paying extra to stay unique!

Love it or loathe it, our custom-built cab is a world

icon and consequently, so are we London cabbies. Many youngsters coming into the trade simply don't realise just how famous we are. This is an example of the extraordinary impact the London taxi has on visiting tourists. A few years back, as Chairman of HALT, I was tentatively involved with a major hotel chain when they conducted a survey in the States, asking potential visitors to London to list their top five 'wannadoes'. Top of the list by far was 'I wanna ride in a *real* London taxi', and a poor second was having an English breakfast of eggs and bacon. If the anti-custom-built cab lobby got their way, will the thousands of visiting tourists ever say they'd 'just lurve to have a ride in an MPV', while eating their egg and bacon?

There are presently dozens of MPVs belonging to reputable PHV companies cruising around the West End going about their legal business of picking up pre-booked fares. Can't you just envisage the disastrous effect on our trade in the future if we were also to plump for MPVs? The only difference between a licensed taxi permitted to ply for hire and, by then, the many thousands of MPVs driven by people who were not allowed to ply for hire, would be a 'For Hire' sign, a taximeter, a Hackney Carriage plate on the back and, probably, a driver who has been fully trained to know where he is going.

Over a period of years, our famous image would become blurred to the public and, eventually, the hands would be raised to hail *any* passing MPV, licensed to ply for hire or otherwise. And if it happens to be very busy and raining, I suspect many of these passengers will be illegally picked up by the PHV drivers. This in turn could well motivate the owners of the PHV companies to challenge our monopoly to 'Ply For Hire' on the grounds that it was 'confusing to the public' and 'hailing any MPV would be a simple solution'. Who knows, this challenge may well occur on an annual basis and eventually some old fart in Whitehall, who had trouble getting a taxi in the pouring rain on Christmas Eve, might agree that it is indeed a simple solution to the constant confusion. And that, my friends, will be that!

These future scenarios are purely hypothetical and based on my speculation and my experience in the trade. Driving a cab in London for some forty years has given me a good living and a deep affection for the freedom of the job, the camaraderie among many of the drivers and the feeling that our history goes back as far as Oliver Cromwell. Not too many people can honestly say, 'I really love my job.' But I can!

I sincerely hope my future scenarios for the trade are so totally wrong that I become a laughing stock among the many people who already know me as 'Mr Doom and Gloom'. But despite all the warning signs, the wide boys in the trade will still continue to turn down the fares going South because of their 'nose bleeds' while passing water! The nightmen will continue to ride around the West End when it's busy, with their 'For Hire' signs switched off, looking for 'clues'. And many of the airport regulars will continue to pay crooked hotel porters a hefty commission to get a job 'up the road'. Their justification has always been that, if they don't pay it, the minicabs soon will. They could be right, but only history will prove it. But don't bet against any of my future scenarios. Continuous apathy and intransigence can destroy anything in this world.

When I first started writing this book, I thought I might dry up after twenty or thirty pages. But not a bit of it. It seems I am blessed with a retentive memory and every happening over my forty years of cabbing – and even before – comes through bright and clear, as though they happened yesterday. I wrote some 50,000 words in just three months and it seems I have only scratched the surface of my memory. Who knows, maybe it could be Edition Number Two of *Cabbie*?

And that, my friends, just about brings us up to date. Thank you kindly for reading my book and I sincerely hope my many American friends get the opportunity to read it. I have a deep affinity with American tourists visiting our great city, because for the past decade or more, I have taken hundreds of these families on two-hour tours, subcontracting from Black Taxi Tours Ltd. They came from just about every state in the Union and I'm positive they will recognise the ugly face smoking a pipe, peering out of the cover, and realise that this indeed was their friend in London for two enjoyable hours.

A very traditional goodbye from a London cabbie reads like this: 'Be lucky, and I wish you long life.'